"PLANTED is a fresh work from someone who loves church planters and works hard for their success. I love the Next Steps sections after each chapter, which leaves no one wondering how to apply the excellent content. This is an excellent resource for those exploring, engaging or encouraging the work of church planting."

Gary Rohrmayer
President of Converge MidAmerica
Author of *Spiritual Conversations*

WHAT OTHERS ARE SAYING

"Read PLANTED! I found it to be a clear, compelling look at ten essential reasons church plants are so effective in reaching others for Jesus. For that reason alone, Jackson has underscored the role of church planting as the 'single most effective evangelistic methodology under heaven.' With lessons, principles and insights from a wealth of experiences in church planting, PLANTED will help any planter—or even a seasoned minister—who is seeking to keep the church focused on the heart of God for those who don't yet know Him."

Mark Batterson
New York Times® best-selling author of *The Circle Maker*

"David Jackson's book originates from a long and constant track record of church planting in environments that are not always friendly to the church. In these pages a church planter will be deeply challenged by both expediency and solid theological underpinnings for the necessity of starting a church through a holistic and culturally effective evangelistic strategy. If you are interested in learning from one of North America's best church planting missiologists – read this book."

Jeff Christopherson
Vice-President, North American Mission Board
Author of *Kingdom Matrix*

"Do you want your church to grow? God does, and so should you. Church growth expert David Jackson believes your church should grow and he shows you the way in PLANTED: Starting Well, Growing Strong. If you are a church planter just getting started, or the pastor of a young church building a foundation, or leading an older church looking for new hope, this book includes insights to empower your church for healthy growth."

Gary L. McIntosh, Ph.D.
Professor of Christian Ministry & Leadership
Talbot School of Theology, Biola University
Author of *There's Hope for Your Church*

"David Jackson's experience and wisdom, gleaned from his years as a church planter and effective church planting leader, is clearly set forth in PLANTED: Starting Well, Growing Strong. Encouraging and practical, with simple and specific next steps makes this especially helpful. It's definitely worth reading and applying his insights."

Dr. Tom Wood
President, Church Multiplication Ministries
Co-Author of *Gospel Coach*

"Forged from the crucible of experience, David Jackson helps your church stay focused on the important task of reaching out and making disciples. PLANTED is a leadership primer to guide church planters, pastors and congregational leaders through the maze of healthy church development that maintains fidelity to the mission of Jesus. Don't miss the 'next steps' at the end of each chapter, especially the powerful questions to process personally and with your team. Prayerfully reflect, carefully plan, and boldly take action."

Robert E. Logan
Author of *The Missional Journey*

"Informed research, testimonies from real practice, and personal anecdotes… you often see one, but seldom see all three blended together so well. The point of PLANTED is this: new churches are more evangelistically effective than older ones, and the reasons why this is so are not really a mystery! God does it, yes, but there are concrete characteristics… they can be named, nurtured, and even applied to existing congregations. David Jackson mines those characteristics, explains and illustrates them, then offers questions and next steps for the reader to use in her/his Church toward embracing and employing them right now. The leader who reads these pages will be drawn toward the heart of Jesus for this world, and the Church who follows that leader will be healthier for it."

Randy Millwood
Author of *To Love and To Cherish from This Day Forward: A Portrait of a Healthy Church*

PLANTED

Starting Well, Growing Strong

J. David Jackson

Screven and Allen Publishing
Severn, Maryland

Copyright © 2012 by J. David Jackson

ISBN-13: 978-0615725390 (Screven and Allen Publishing)
ISBN-10: 0615725392

All rights reserved. Printed in the United States of America. No part of this book may be used or reproduced in any manner whatsoever without written permission except in the case of brief quotations embodied in critical articles and reviews.

Printed in the United States of America

Unless otherwise noted, all Scripture quotations are taken from the Holman Christian Standard Bible®, Copyright © 1999, 2000, 2002, 2003, 2009 by Holman Bible Publishers. Used by permission. Holman Christian Standard Bible®, Holman CSB®, and HCSB® are federally registered trademarks of Holman Bible Publishers.

Cover photo: © Artist: Rebekah Jackson, 2012
Cover design: © Artist: Jonathan Jackson, 2013

DEDICATION

*To the love of my life,
my wife and partner in church planting,
Joyce Jackson,
God's greatest gift to me:
You make every single day
an adventure worth living*

ACKNOWLEDGEMENTS

A book like this becomes reality only because a team of people I know and love have joined me in the process. My family is certainly at the top of such a list. My wife, Joye, has helped me with the manuscript in many ways, offering wise suggestions and sound, creative advice. My children, Sarah, Jonathan and Rebekah, have each contributed to the content and presentation you see here. Many thanks go out to each of them for their investment in me and in the work that is before you.

Others have helped with the editorial efforts for the book. A handful of colleagues and friends have contributed ideas, corrections and critiques to help this book become better in its final form. Earl, my coach and advocate through the entire process, has been an invaluable source of wisdom, patience and support. I offer my thanks to Randy, Jack, Mark, Shannon and Sharon for your labors on my behalf. Dan, you went out on a limb for me with the publication of this book; thanks for trusting me enough to write the foreword and put your name on this effort. Additional colleagues have affirmed my work through their endorsements and encouragement along the way; their comments are included in the material here. My father, James T. Jackson, deserves special recognition for his detailed analysis, observations and assistance in rounding this manuscript into shape.

To the nearly four hundred church planters who've been a part of the journey, I express my gratitude. Much of what is found here, I have learned from you. Your experiences and friendship have taught me so much and have enabled our church planting ministry to become more effective over the years. The Baptist Convention of Maryland/Delaware and the Greater Boston Baptist Association in New England has given me the privilege of serving them in church multiplication over the past two decades; I am thankful for their support and the freedom to think outside the box to assist our planters in reaching more people for Jesus.

I am thankful for the lives of William Screven, first Baptist church planter to the South—departing from Maine and heading to South Carolina during the colonial period to begin the First Baptist Church of Charleston—and of Roland Allen, Anglican missionary to China, whose books on church planting missionary methods have influenced tens of thousands, including me. Their names and examples have shaped the work of the company that is publishing this book.

Most of all, I am thankful to the Lord Jesus Christ, for saving my soul and calling me into service for Him. The past twenty-two years in church planting ministry have been awe-inspiring, humbling and exhilarating beyond belief. Through it all God has shown immeasurable grace and mercy to me and given me the incredible opportunity to partner with Him in some small way to extend His Kingdom. For that, I am, and will always be, eternally grateful.

J. David Jackson
March 1, 2013

TABLE OF CONTENTS

Foreword by Dan Kimball   xiii

Introduction   1
- Sovereignty and Partnership
- Experience is a Great Teacher
- What the Research Shows
- Not All Growth is the Same Kind of Growth
- The Thesis of This Book
- "You Are Here"

Chapter 1: An Inspiring Leader   13
- Pro-Active Visionary
- Momentum is Essential
- A General and A Cheerleader
- Faith, Hope and Love
- Power in Prayer
- Man in the Mirror
- *Next Steps*

Chapter 2: Calling and Motivation   27
- Calling
- Personality
- Proper Motivation
- Success and Failure
- Desperation
- *Next Steps*

Chapter 3: Vision and Focus   39
- Pulled Forward
- Stewardship of Vision
- Single-Mindedness
- Simple Church
- Warning! Danger Ahead
- *Next Steps*

Chapter 4: Passion for Those without Jesus   51
- Lost People Matter to Them
- Advocacy
- Planning with Them in Mind
- Relevance
- *Next Steps*

Chapter 5: Creativity and Innovation   63
- Creativity
- "Right-Brained" Activity
- Youth-like
- Bridges and Barriers
- *Next Steps*

Chapter 6: The Power of Relationships   75
- People More than Programs
- Informal Gatherings
- Limited Structure
- Word-of-Mouth Marketing
- *Next Steps*

Chapter 7: Kingdom Citizens   87
- Loyalty and Brand Names
- Big-Picture Perspective
- Cooperative around the Larger Mission
- Creative Alliances
- *Next Steps*

Chapter 8: Budget and Time Priorities   99
- Around Mission
- Evangelism and Outreach
- Missions Involvement
- Fixed Expenses
- *Next Steps*

Chapter 9: In the Community   113
- Know Your Community
- Go, not Come (Only) Strategy
- Social Gospel?
- Earning Credibility
- Serving as Well as Sharing
- *Next Steps*

Chapter 10: Limited Structure   125
- K.I.S.S. (aka, Less is More)
- Family or Business?
- To Bless or to Curse?
- Placement, Not Nomination or Election
- *Next Steps*

Epilogue   137
- Next Steps for Church Plants
- Next Steps for Established Churches

FOREWORD

Oh, if I would have had this book to read before I planted a church!

I am a church planter. So for me, reading this book is like listening to someone who knew exactly what I had experienced and the questions with which I had grappled during my early planting days. From my personal experience of planting a church, it is amazing to see how incredibly familiar David is with the process and stages of church planting about which he writes here. That's what makes this book stand out from others.

The more I read books and talk to authors, the more I discover there are those who write about theories of church leadership and church planting – but it is only theory. Their words haven't gone through the test of time or real world experience. This reality always makes me take into account the author when reading church planting or leadership books; I want to make sure they actually are genuine practitioners.

David is just that. And as long as I have known him, he has been a student of church planting. He has planted churches personally. He teaches church planters. He learns from church planters. I see him on the Internet posting about his meetings with church planters. Church planting is in his blood and distinguishes his life. If you want to understand church planting, David is a writer who you will want to get to know.

I had the privilege of speaking at a conference that David hosted a few years ago. It took place in his local area, so the people who came to the conference already knew him. It was obvious that the church planters and leaders there had tremendous respect for him. How unusual it is to find a prophet who is respected in his own town! This speaks volumes. When you see that the planters with whom David works closely respect him, you can know that his writing will go beyond theoretical ideas and will provide reliable resources for planting and growing healthy churches. This book delivers that and more.

I don't want to overview what is in the book here, as you will have the joy of reading what is ahead on your own. But what I do want to say is that this book is a much needed one. There are a couple of reasons for this. First, the author is experienced and trusted in the world of church planting, as I have already emphasized. Secondly, there is an urgency you will sense from this book that pinpoints the need to do whatever it takes to see people come to know who Jesus is and in response, to follow Him. David stresses that urgency. We can't just go on doing church as usual, for eternal lives are at stake.

Well-known London preacher Charles Spurgeon wrote,

> *If sinners be damned, at least let them leap to Hell over our dead bodies. And if they perish, let them perish with our arms wrapped about their knees, imploring them to stay. If Hell must be filled, let it be filled in the teeth of our exertions, and let not one go unwarned and unprayed for.*

This is why church planting is important.

We must take risks to reach the world for Jesus. Church planting is both faith-stretching and risky, but with the right guidance, it doesn't have to be quite so risky. It will be faith-stretching, no matter what. So, I know that if I were thinking of planting a church, I would want as much practical help as possible. In this book you are about to read one of the most inspiring and practical guides for church planters I know. I read it through and I got so excited about church planting, I wanted to plant another church!

May God use this book to encourage and equip those who are thinking of church planting, as well as those who have done so and need further guidance. I am excited to think that, as a result of this book, those reading will learn and be inspired about church planting. And they, in turn, will hopefully see those who don't know Jesus yet come to know Him.

As I type this concluding thought, I am praying for you who are reading this book and for those who will come to know Jesus because of the churches you plant.

Dan Kimball
Vintage Faith Church, founding pastor
Santa Cruz, California
Author of *Adventures in Churchland*
April, 2013

PLANTED
Starting Well, Growing Strong

Introduction

Pastor Joe paused to catch his breath. The first anniversary celebration of Redemption Fellowship was finally over, but not before a daylong series of festivities had been completed. Over a hundred and fifty people had shown up, few who a year ago would have even known the others present and a large majority who twelve months prior had not claimed the name of Jesus.

This new family of believers certainly had much to celebrate. Pastor Joe had relocated here from upstate and had renewed relationships with key city leaders in this town where he had lived as a child. The church of Pastor Joe's youth had been supportive of his efforts, sending people and money to encourage the new work. He and his key leaders had led dozens of men and women to the Lord, evidencing the preparatory work of God in that place and further confirming to Pastor Joe that he was where God had called and placed him. A day of worship with many first-time visitors also suggested God's blessing upon the ministry.

Everyone who was a part of Redemption Fellowship had labored hard, doing yeoman's work and tirelessly sacrificing for the cause. Their efforts certainly contributed to the difference already evident in the fledgling congregation and now beginning to be seen in the community at large.

Pastor Joe marveled at the way God was using him in this church planting effort. Two years ago, if you'd asked him where he was headed in ministry, church planting would not have been on his radar. God, however, had other plans. Looking back, the young church planter thought, "I can see how the Heavenly Father prepared me for this work. I guess Rick Warren is right when he reminds us all: 'God doesn't waste any experience.'[1]

"And now, the church has taken root and has started to grow," Joe continued. "So many things threatened its survival and challenged its viability during this first year. Yet God has kept us on mission and has led us every step of the way."

Pastor Joe had been asked frequently how they had made so much progress in such a short amount of time. The church planter knew there were many factors involved. The focus on evangelism was essential. And, of course, there were crossroads moments and decisions made that were crucial. However, in the final analysis, Joe relied on 1 Corinthians 3:6 for his answer: "I planted, Apollos watered, but God gave the growth."

"Now that Redemption Fellowship is off to a good start," Joe concluded, "we need to make sure that it stays healthy and grows strong. Our future—in God's hands—depends upon it."

My wife, Joye, is a gardener. An amateur gardener, to be sure, but she aspires to more. She finds great joy and satisfaction in selecting the flowers and vegetables to plant, working the soil, getting her hands dirty and, of course, seeing the "fruit" of her labor.

All gardeners know that every plant has to have various elements to thrive. The environment is critical. There needs to be good topsoil, free of rocks and debris. Nutrients are necessary: water, air and sunlight are needed in the right amounts. Threats have to be minimized: fences or chicken wire might be needed to protect the plants from natural predators. Work has to be done: the soil needs to be tilled and prepared for the planting of seeds at just the right depth. Commitment has to be seen: growth has to be monitored and plans adjusted to meet surfacing needs.

In the best of scenarios, these insights and actions can help a plant to develop as it should. But in the final analysis, only God in His sovereignty can enable it to grow. He does the "invisible" work on the seed that brings it to life for the world to see.

This book is about the elements that God uses to cause new churches like Redemption Fellowship to grow. My assumption is that if you're reading this book, you have a desire for your church to grow, no matter whether you're a new church or an old one. If you're considering church planting, you'll want to discover the secrets to an exceptional church plant. If you are already a church planter in the field for a year or two, then you'll want to be reminded of what made your church so effective in the first place. This is important so that you don't lose the principles that were implemented and resulted in such extraordinary growth. And if you're an established church, especially one over fifteen years of age, then the "good news" is that if you're willing to implement these strategies, then your church, too, can grow like it did in those early years.

SOVEREIGNTY AND PARTNERSHIP

The apostle Paul reminds us that God causes His church "plants" to grow. I agree wholeheartedly! He is a sovereign God and no one steals any of His glory or honor. He is incomparable and all-powerful. And as a sovereign Almighty God, He has the right and ability to do whatever He chooses to do, and that includes the way He grows His church. Yet, He gives us the opportunity to partner with Him in this work of planting His church, much like the gardener who partners with the Creator to see flowers and fruit grow to maturity. Amazingly, God invites us into this process with Him.

Surely gardeners are fully aware that they can't "make" anything grow, but they also know that they have a part to play in this agricultural process. In fact, over time they learn that there are principles and characteristics that are typical of good gardening. They know the seasons of the year make a difference and that there are various ways to test the soil. They understand that they have to be dedicated to the work, especially at certain junctures in the process. They have a desire to enable each plant to have the best chance for success by providing every advantage they can for its development. However, in the end they realize God controls the results.

As church planters, God also controls the results. Yet He gives us a part to play in this process. Like Paul, many of us have been called to plant; others, to water. We join God in the adventure of seeing new churches sprout and come to life!

What an awesome joy and privilege that is; what a tremendous responsibility it is, as well. And if you are like me, you strive to be the best gardener you can be for our Lord. You want to know how to cultivate the environment, to plant the seed effectively and to enable it to experience His miraculous growth into the future. You want to plant with wisdom and insight; to lean on the experiences of planters who've gone before and to glean the factors that contributed to their effectiveness.

> I'll tell you the "Miracle Gro®" secret right up front: evangelism. In fact, all of these elements will have limited or meaningless impact unless they are married to evangelism.

This book can help you with that. In fact, I feel so strongly about the need for this wisdom that out of my experience I've compiled ten key characteristics that effective new churches have applied in their "planting," which have contributed to their success. Planters who have applied these elements have started well during their first few years. Over time, these factors have also helped them grow stronger and healthier as the new church matured. But I'll tell you the "Miracle Gro®" secret right up front: evangelism. In fact, all of these elements will have limited or meaningless impact unless they are married to evangelism. It is the single most significant ingredient that enables church plants to grow so well.

EXPERIENCE IS A GREAT TEACHER

In my ministry, three times I've been involved in planting a church. I've watched the early years of strong and sometimes explosive growth. The exhilaration and euphoria that it brings are unmatched in ministry! One day there is no one there; within months, there is a congregation of fifty or a hundred. Perhaps there is no other time in the life of a church that will match the percentage of growth that takes place during the first couple of years. Of course, with that growth comes a sense of impact; the new church is making a difference!

People are saved.

Lives are changed.

Marriages are rescued.

The hope and belief is that ultimately communities will be transformed by the power and grace of Jesus Christ Himself.

The by-products of such impact for the new church are enormous. Unity is strengthened. Leadership is enhanced. Outreach is magnified. Ownership and participation in the life of the church grows. You find yourself wondering if you should ask someone to pinch you, just to make sure this isn't a dream. You don't want it to end, because you feel successful in what God has called you there to do.

On the other hand, I've seen the opposite side of ministry too, working in two settings where struggle and decline were the norm. In these instances, with hard work and congregational commitment, both situations turned around and began growing again. Many of the keys we write about here were put into effect in these settings, and they made an impact. We were determined not to leave any of our God-given potential "on the cutting room floor."

Over the years I've also served as a temporary leader in no less than fourteen other churches as a transitional, interim pastor. They have ranged in size from thirty-five to around seven hundred. They have been young, in their first three years, and old, dating back to the 1950s. Granted they were all in a time of transition, but each was either plateaued in terms of their own growth or exhibited warning signs suggesting difficulty could be ahead. To be honest, getting a church to grow in this scenario is often the hardest of all, due to the interim nature of ministry and the fact that those closest to the fire often don't even see it.

What made these churches grow, or in some of these interim situations, not grow? The answer emphatically was their degree of commitment to evangelism.

WHAT THE RESEARCH SHOWS

Perhaps you're thinking by now that all of this is just the whimsical perspective of a guy who has spent years in a select number of churches but has no clue about the world where you live. If that is what you're thinking, then I'd be the first to agree with you. That's why the words of Dr. C. Peter Wagner at the beginning of chapter one in *Church Planting for a Greater Harvest* (1990) are so important. In his definitive book on church planting, Wagner wrote, "The single most effective evangelistic methodology under heaven is planting new churches." It is the most-often quoted statement about the importance of church planting in my lifetime. What's even more amazing about it is that Wagner, then professor from Fuller Theological Seminary, chose not to footnote it, though he stated that it "has been well-substantiated by research over the past two or three decades." As he proceeded, he failed to share with his audience the research to which he was referring, giving no more than anecdotal illustrations of this great truth. He just boldly proclaimed its significance and value, then moved on to present the process for how to plant a new church in the remainder of the book.[2]

Needless to say, Wagner's comment caught the eye of many church growth specialists and publications over the ensuing years. Were church plants really better at evangelism? Did they really grow more effectively in evangelism than long-established churches? Where was the evidence to back up such an audacious claim?

Christianity Today magazine was the first to produce new documentation for his statement. Early the next year, they wrote that in fact, just as Wagner had suggested, new churches do indeed grow much faster than older churches—actually, more than three times faster. They found that for every one hundred members in the church, new churches under three years of age saw ten new believers come to faith in Christ, compared to three new believers per one hundred members for churches older than fifteen years of age.[3]

The American Society for Church Growth followed suit close to the end of the decade. In a report presented to the Executive Presbytery, they found similar evidence for church plants: if a church is less than three years old, it takes only three people to lead one person to Christ. This study found those reached in established churches to be dramatically lower, at a ratio of 1:85 for churches over ten years of age.[4]

The Southern Baptist Convention took up the same question in 2000, studying its own 43,000-plus churches to see what the research showed among its own congregations. This study, too, found Wagner's original statement to be accurate. The ratio of 1:10 for new churches remained the same, while for established churches, it was considerably higher (1:29 for churches age 21-30 and 1:47 for churches over the age of fifty),[5] though not as high as that reported by the American Society for Church Growth.

Lest the reader think all these studies are old news and not valid today, the evidence continues. The *Natural Church Development* research project done by Christian Schwartz, Aubrey Malphurs and Ed Stetzer in their comprehensive books on church planting and even the North American Mission Board's website in 2012 cite research that promote the same findings.[6] Since the North American Mission Board's information is the most current, it is referenced here. In declaring the evangelistic effectiveness of church planting, it states, "Southern Baptist churches baptized 3.4 people per 100 resident members, while new churches baptized 11.7,"[7] again

> Just as Wagner had suggested, new churches do indeed grow much faster than older churches—actually, more than three times faster.

suggesting that new churches are over three times more effective evangelistically than older, established churches.

The conclusion is obvious: new church plants are more evangelistic on a per capita basis. This number is especially high when they are younger, and axiomatically, smaller. No less than Tim Keller has said:

> The vigorous, continual planting of new congregations is the single most crucial strategy for 1) the numerical growth of the Body of Christ in any city, and 2) the continual corporate renewal and revival of the existing churches in a city. Nothing else—not crusades, outreach programs, parachurch ministries, growing mega-churches, congregational consulting, nor church renewal processes—will have the consistent impact of dynamic, extensive church planting. This is an eyebrow raising statement. But to those who have done any study at all, it is not even controversial.[8]

NOT ALL GROWTH IS THE SAME KIND OF GROWTH

But not all growth is evangelistic. Churches of all ages and sizes grow by virtue of transfer growth, too. Families and individuals change churches as a result of the increased mobility in our society. However, they also move their membership because of conflict with a current church's leadership or its programming, or even worse, simply due to the consumeristic attitude the church members in large part have adopted.

Church plants are not immune to this kind of growth. Transfer growth can happen in the best of circumstances when a parent or sponsoring church sends out members to be a part of the fledgling ministry's initial core. This adds stability, leadership and maturity to the new church's early efforts. But other church hoppers and shoppers will join the typical new church, too, and frankly, many new churches appeal to them through marketing strategies and programming options they offer.

To be sure, this kind of growth is not all bad, but it is deceptive. Many churches within denominations, for example, grow in number only because of transfer growth. Such churches may give the appearance of numerical growth, but in fact, they are participating in only a "reshuffling of the deck." Such growth may help one church and hurt another, but does nothing to grow the Kingdom of God.

Evangelistic growth—often called conversion growth—is different. While it can be subdivided into those who are converted with familial connections to the church and those who have no such connections, evangelistic growth differs in that it is adding people to the Kingdom, not just moving them around from one place to another. New churches have the potential to be highly effective at this for a variety of reasons that this book will explore. Yet, even this growth, with its raw evangelistic fervor, becomes tempered in the life of the new church by year four. This makes it more imperative than ever that we come to understand the dynamics that make these early years so successful in growth.

THE THESIS OF THIS BOOK

In a word, this book strives to show the reader why new churches grow so quickly and effectively in their early years. The assumption is that once known, these principles can be adapted and implemented in churches of any age, with the result being greater conversion growth. While the principles are transferable to any setting, the dynamics of each individual church, including its community, its leadership and often its age, will make the application of these principles varied and the results, different. Most older churches cannot expect a conversion growth rate of thirty-three percent a year, as found in the youngest of churches, but all churches ought to be able to increase their growth rate by five to ten percent, even in their first year of implementation.

For that to happen, churches have to understand what makes a new work like "Redemption Fellowship" tick. They have to see behind the visible activities to what enables the new church to make decisions, budget strategically, engage people so effectively and see so many people come to know Jesus as Savior and Lord. Once seen, established churches have to examine their own situation and grapple with things like identity and purpose, programming and facilities. They also have to confront barriers that hinder their growth, like community perception, history and structure. Then, bottom line, they must want to reverse the trend or get off the plateau badly enough to make the necessary changes for growth to happen.

> Planters need to be reminded early to "keep the main thing, the main thing." Otherwise, they will find themselves in the same boat as older churches and never even realize what happened when it begins to sink.

Church plants are not exempt from the danger of losing their evangelistic zeal. In fact, almost all of them eventually do within their first decade of existence. Time and again I deal with church planters who long for the day when they can enjoy all the amenities that a "full service church" experiences. Yet they fail to realize that those very amenities often plant the seeds that create the hindrances to growth down the road. Planters need to be reminded early to "keep the main thing, the main thing." Otherwise, they will find themselves in the same boat as older churches and never even realize what happened when it begins to sink.

This book shares ten keys to unlocking the potential in every church plant, and by extension, any church—young or old—that will apply them within its own setting. Each of these keys is a part of the story behind the evangelistic fervor and effectiveness of church plants. Some of the keys are internal within the mind and heart of the new community of faith. We will look at things like calling, vision, creativity and structure. We will analyze their impact on the outward activity of the church. In essence, we will seek to answer the question, "Why do new churches do what they do?"

Some of these keys, though, are external, seen in action and behavior that result from the difference in internal makeup and perspective. We will investigate elements like outreach, relationships, connection with the community and focus on the Kingdom. We will see how these new churches tap into their potential and apply themselves to the opportunities they have to maximize their limited resources and reach those without Christ so effectively. In these chapters, we will attempt to answer the question, "What do new churches do?"

Perhaps a few other words about the book's format are in order at this point. Each chapter will begin with a case study involving the hypothetical church introduced earlier in this introduction, "Redemption Fellowship," and its church planting leader, Pastor Joe. This case study is given in an attempt to help the reader visualize the issue or concern being addressed in the forthcoming chapter. The chapters will also end with a *"Next Steps"* section, which will include ways to apply that particular characteristic within your own setting, big questions in need of answers and places to dig deeper into this topic, if desired.

"YOU ARE HERE"

This book is not linear in format. You can read any section, any topic, in any order. Whatever benefits you most <u>now</u> should determine for you where you start and what content you read. The intent is the information here will meet you at your congregation's point of need.

A final word is in order: I love the church. In fact, at times I've been convicted that I love the church too much, even rivaling my love for our Lord Himself. (I'm working on this.) I love the church in all its myriad shapes and sizes, ages and forms. I've been a part of many kinds of churches; through my current ministry, I've been blessed to participate in many, many more. I am a big fan of the church. I believe in it; I support it. I know it to be God's Kingdom agent in our world. When it is fulfilling its potential, there is nothing like it! There is no substitute for the Bride of Christ.

I tell you this, because at times in this book my words may sound harsh or critical. I don't mean them to be. And I don't mean it to be personal in the sense you take offense at what I say. Sure, there are times you will disagree with me; maybe even get angry at my statements. That's okay. It will likely help us learn more together. But what you need to hear me say is I speak because I care. I care a lot. I have not written off the church…far from it.

I simply hope and pray my vantage point in viewing the life and development of the church can help others learn from those around them, so that every church, no matter what age, can enjoy the fullness of God's plan for them.

1

An Inspiring Leader

Pastor Joe was convinced God had called him to plant a church. In fact, he was so sure of it that even when the placement office at his seminary contacted him about other ministry opportunities available to him after graduation, he declined. He was determined to see this church planting project through to the end; there was no turning back.

As a "doer" in life, Joe sought ways to act upon his understanding of the vision God was revealing to him. He dreamed big dreams, played out in his head many "what if" situations and did what he felt necessary to prepare himself for such possibilities down the road. He spent time developing relationships with churches and parachurch organizations that believed in Joe and the ministry he was readying himself to do. One by one several of them became partners with Pastor Joe in the soon-to-be-planted church.

Joe also prayed for understanding in regards to where and among whom God was directing him to start this new church. He knew that "need" was everywhere—some places and peoples were obviously more needy than others—but he determined to look also for signs where "God was at work already" and was inviting Joe to join Him there. This principle of receptivity brought responsiveness in the community where God eventually led Pastor Joe to live and serve. Evidence of progress—large or small—encouraged Joe and the fledgling group of people who were forming a nucleus of the new church-to-be. He knew building on this momentum would encourage others to join with the group, too, and would also serve to propel the ministry forward in a positive way.

If you knew Pastor Joe, you'd be impressed by his conviction and passion right away. He is strong-willed and tenacious in his determination. He projects a strong faith in his God, a steely confidence in the future and a genuine love for the people He knows. He is the "eternal optimist" when it comes to God and is able, almost always, to inspire others to believe the same. Make no mistake, when the group is together he can challenge them and they seem ready to overcome whatever obstacle is in their way.

You'd be impressed with his evangelistic zeal, too. He is always ready to "give an answer for the hope that is within him," if given the chance. He loves to share the Good News of Jesus Christ with anyone who will afford him the opportunity. He does this because he truly loves God and the people whom God has sent him to reach. In fact, he lives a life of evangelism so relational and so evident to others that many in the new church have already started following his example through their lives, too.

Try as you may, you can't get away from this incontrovertible fact: leadership is critical in determining the ever-expanding impact of any organization. If a group of people has empowered a person to cast vision and give direction, that person will have a direct bearing upon the work and influence of this same group of people. In addition, if the leader is effective, he or she will cast a much larger net of impact upon the community at large and extend the shadow of the organization far beyond its literal walls.

Churches are the same. A church planter or a pastor, depending upon the polity and structure employed, will have varying degrees of influence upon the Body of Christ and its ministry. Yet, as a leader, no one in the congregation will carry more impact than that church planter (and very few—if any—will have more influence in an established church than its equivalent pastor).

John Maxwell has reminded us that "leadership IS influence."[9] In this day and age, that influence is earned through the credibility of one's life and seen in the character and competency with which one lives. No longer is credibility simply granted to someone because that person has a title or position, a certain education or experience. Leadership is earned day-to-day, person-by-person.

Churches, like all organizations, have leaders, beginning with the pastor. However, successful church plants have a certain caliber of leader, capable of inspiring others to believe in the unseen and to attempt the impossible. His ability to inspire—not just direct or navigate the affairs of the church and its people—sets him apart from those who pastor a large percentage of established churches. He is truly a leader and not a manager.

Effective church planters lead in outreach and inspire through evangelism. They live among the people of the community, loving them to Jesus and seeking to share the life-changing Gospel message with them in any way they can. This is a lifestyle for such planters and inspires others to learn and share, to discover and take risks, in order that more people can come to know the Good News, too. They realize that their leadership is more caught than taught. As a result, their example, along with their values and passions, carry great weight on the future of the church plant and its newly-forming DNA.

PRO-ACTIVE VISIONARY

Church planters are visionaries. They see the big picture. They dream big dreams. For them, the dream is not just about numbers or buildings. The vision effective planters embrace is risk-taking and potentially world-changing. We will talk more about vision in a later chapter, but here it is best to say that the vision captures the leader; he is owned by it. He eats it; he sleeps it. It invades his every moment, so much so that he cannot "push it to the side." It requires his immediate and constant attention.

Since effective church planters are self-starters—doers by nature—this is not a hard step for planters to take. They are all about seeing the dream come true. In fact, hardly a day will go by in which the planter fails to engage the vision and attempt through his behavior and activity to bring it one step closer to reality. The vision will compel him to act upon it.

This pro-active nature brings with it a sense of immediacy and urgency. Planters will want to flesh out the vision fully and effectively, but quickly...not in days or weeks, but in years, not decades. They have a sense of necessity about them, much like the Scriptures tell us of Jesus (e.g., *"He had to travel through Samaria,"* John 4:4, where "had to" translates a Greek verb, *dei*, that commentators call "the divine imperative").[10]

Busyness is not the goal, to be sure, but activity is an ally in moving people into service. Stated in the opposite way, a corporate life in the church that is sedentary and passive does not engender vision fulfillment. It does not get members off the sidelines and into ministry. But a passionate, inspired leader moves people into action through his example and his determination...and positive, forward-moving activity creates momentum.

MOMENTUM IS ESSENTIAL

In the earliest months of a new church plant's existence, there is an intangible enemy that confronts it: ignorance. No one in the community knows of the new church's existence, save for the planter and the few committed people who make up its initial core. That small group of people must overcome the ignorance of others by making their presence known among the townspeople.

As a result, they "attack" issues and concerns together as a new congregation where they can make a difference and affect change for the better among individuals, family and the community at large. This is done through the power of the Gospel and the love of Christ, which compels them into action. Effective church planters want to harness this energy, so that it will grow. They lead the group in ways through which they can succeed and at the same time begin to accomplish parts of the vision. Accomplishment that leads to victory creates momentum.

Momentum cannot be overestimated in its value to a new church plant.

It generates excitement among the people.
It emboldens them to take more chances.
It grows their faith.
It fuels their evangelistic zeal.
It facilitates impact in the community.
It begins to erase the ignorance of others about the new church that has started.

The recently concluded Space Shuttle program in the United States taught us the importance of momentum. NASA tells us that the majority of the fuel needed for the Space Shuttle is used up in the first few minutes of its mission.[11] Why? It is because the Shuttle has to generate momentum against the gravity of the earth that would prefer it to "stay at rest." An inspiring leader recognizes the need to "push against gravity" in the early days. He understands this takes a lot of energy and effort. He realizes the need to fight against a sedentary existence, without activity or effort. He also knows that once the momentum builds, it will soon come to a place where it will fuel itself forward, much like the proverbial snowball headed downhill.

A GENERAL AND A CHEERLEADER

An inspiring leader will intuitively know the advantage he has and the credibility he gains when activity leads to success. Motivation becomes internalized; momentum encourages further activity. Accomplishment validates the effort and brings fulfillment to those who are a part of the journey.

Every victory adds to credibility. Credibility leads to legitimacy. Inspiration becomes easier because it is experienced and eventually owned by those who now share it.

In these days, effective church planters inspire the people in their congregation through two primary roles, that of a general and that of a cheerleader. While the juxtaposition of these two roles may surprise some readers, the integrated characteristics of both can easily be seen and understood. An inspiring leader can now truly and legitimately lead with others who will follow, much as a general does by virtue of his earned and acknowledged authority. The planter directs the new church plant; he leads believers to grow as disciples. He paints big and challenging objectives for the church to engage, and at the same time he marshals the resources needed to achieve them. He keeps the congregation united and focused and he enables them to "see" and acknowledge a clearly defined enemy. The better he can do these things, the better he will be able to use the momentum that has been created to his advantage.

At the same time, an inspiring leader will be the number one cheerleader for his congregation. He will "rally the troops" through his belief in them, expressed often and in clear terms, like "I believe in you" or "I love our church." He will exude joy publicly in the opportunity God has given him to lead this new church. He will celebrate the accomplishments of the one and of the many. He will revel in the difference the new church is making for Jesus. The planter will urge the congregation to even greater victory, out of his belief in our great God, to the vision they must achieve and the value of the people within the family.

John Woods is a church planter who perfectly illustrates this. In the summertime, Woods began his church plant where he had grown up on the eastern shore of Maryland. As a native of the area and with many long-time relationships, John was able to move quicker than most toward a public launch of Bayside Community Church in weekly worship. The church plant started services before Christmas and immediately starting reaching extraordinarily high numbers of town residents. By Easter they had almost doubled those in attendance again. They ended their first year with fifty-one first-time followers of Jesus Christ added to their new church family.

Why? Well, clearly God is blessing Bayside with His presence and power. But Pastor John is also the inspiring leader-type, who is both a general and a cheerleader. He is deliberate and focused. He has mapped out a plan for success. He is pro-active in leading the people and refuses to "do it all," instead delegating to his "lieutenants" various responsibilities that must be done. He is also constantly exhorting his people on to greater heights by challenging them to keep looking forward and not to be satisfied with what they've experienced so far. In addition, he is always using words and actions, in person and through social media, to tell them how much he loves the church and being their pastor.

FAITH, HOPE AND LOVE

That's inspired leadership. Planters like John are not your typical American ministers in the twenty-first century. Extremely effective church planters project an extraordinary faith in God. Whether out of naïveté or refined by the trials of experience, they genuinely believe that God still moves mountains and can make the impossible become reality. They are audacious in the claims they are willing to make on God's behalf and tenacious in clinging to the belief that He will obliterate what others would perceive as impenetrable obstacles in the way. They personify the words of the writer of Hebrews, *"Now without faith it is impossible to please God, for the one who draws near to Him must believe that He exists and rewards those who seek Him"* (Hebrews 11:6). The fact that these leaders rarely lack in faith inspires others who struggle in this regard, especially when they

> They live by the words of William Carey who said, "Expect great things from God; attempt great things for God."

see evidence of God at work in and through such leaders. Faith breeds more faith.

These planters also are fans of the future. They believe it truly is a preferred place to be. Many of them "live there." They are attracted to it, optimistic about it and ever moving intentionally toward it. They long for it and are eager to see it come to fruition. These planter-leaders are filled with hope and expectancy, endued with the conviction that God has better things ahead. They live by the words of William Carey who said, "Expect great things from God; attempt great things for God."[12] Their hopefulness engenders confidence in others about the future, too, if for no other reason than to realize that with such a leader and church, one never will have to face that future alone.

Inspiring leaders also exhibit a genuine love for God and others. They are often open and transparent about their relationships, strengths and weaknesses. While acknowledging relationships are often messy, the sincere love and devotion shown and evident to members of the congregation inspire them to work out their relationships in love, too. Their authenticity encourages others in their own relationships, whether in good times or bad. Such love bonds people together, elicits support when needed and transcends circumstances, even in the face of conflict. Few other things inspire people to grow and serve more than unconditional love.

POWER IN PRAYER

The inspiring leader's genuine love for God is evident in his prayer life. While most church planters are not typically the reflective, meditative type, effective ones are passionate about the power of prayer, personally and corporately. They pray throughout the day and know the need of blocking out time to spend with God. While they are "on the go" doers, they still find time and ways to cultivate and enhance their own walk with God and to mine the depth of communing with Him.

Their impassioned prayers before the congregation are both personal and inspiring, as they reveal elements of the relationship the leader has with his God and the faith, hope and love he exhibits in his life. This honesty and enthusiasm heard by others also finds its way into their hearts, challenging them as well to be more open and heartfelt with their Savior and Lord.

While prayer could easily be another element why new churches grow, church planters (and pastors, too, for that matter) know there is power in prayer that cannot be replaced with anything else. This characteristic is certainly essential to the well-being and effectiveness of godly leaders, but not necessarily exclusive to them. Some believers would no doubt be classified quantitatively as greater pray-ers than the effective church planters we reference here. In fact, my personal experience is the greatest prayer warriors I've known have been in the pews, not the pulpit. Regardless, planters understand, value and live out dependence on God in prayer. They surround themselves with dozens, if not hundreds, of others who pray passionately and consistently for them and their ministry.

They know that there is no lasting power without prayer.

MAN IN THE MIRROR

The impact of the inspiring leader shows itself in another remarkable way. We have noted that over time, leaders both through their modeling and their teaching influence the behavior of those in their congregations. In point of fact, a more accurate way of saying this might be that individuals in the congregation will begin to "mirror" the inspiring leader who has greatly inspired them. Their values will become similar, their actions more predictable. The example of the leader will be emulated by those who follow and

> His ability to "imprint" the new church's attitudes and actions has huge ramifications, and it demands sober responsibility from the leader himself.

hold him in high regard, similar to but not nearly as conscious as the efforts of a child with a parent.

In church plants this typically takes place by the second birthday of the new church; in established churches, it takes several more years, due to the "layers" of previous pastor-leaders the church has had. This reality makes longevity a valuable commodity in any church's life, and it increases the value of the truly inspiring leader in a new church plant. His ability to "imprint" the new church's attitudes and actions has huge ramifications, and it demands sober responsibility from the leader himself.

Evangelism and discipleship are a major part of what he models well for the new church. Effective church planters will live in such a way that they discover, engage and build relationships with those who do not yet know Jesus. (More about this will be addressed in a later chapter.) They will share with them the difference Jesus makes and typically lead many into an eternal, life-changing relationship with Him. This "grows" the new church family and also models for those already there what an evangelistic lifestyle of God's love for others can look like in them.

Because the DNA of the new church is set within the formative years of the church, these early years in development will be played out over and over again through the life of the congregation. If the church planter is evangelistic, the church will become evangelistic. If he is full of faith, hope and love, the new church will be also. If he in turn is an inspiring leader, it will create from within the congregation other inspiring leaders who will multiply the impact and influence of the church planter, possibly for decades to come.

Likely, this will lead the congregation to seek other future inspiring leaders, when needed. In addition, it won't just happen in the original church itself. More importantly, with time it will also spread "wide," through other church plants, mission endeavors and even relocated members, who will carry with them the DNA to inspire others as they lead God's people in service.

John Maxwell, in his devotional book *Leadership Lessons for Every Day*, suggests that a leader who lives a typical lifetime will impact at least 10,000 persons.[13] If this is genuinely true, perhaps there is no other reason why new churches are more effective, now and in the future unfolding of their ministries, than this. Effective planters inspire many others who, in turn, are able to do the same.

NEXT STEPS

APPLY TO YOUR SETTING

Evaluate the leadership in your own church plant. The place to start is with an intentional and honest "reality check." Look for evidence of the characteristics mentioned here in your own church setting. Then, major on your strengths; minimize your weaknesses.

Create greater momentum for the new church. Determine how to do this in both attitude and action.

Pray over your leaders and core group members. Maxwell says you should spend eighty percent of your time with them.[14] As you think about these key people, discern who needs you to be "a general" for them today and who needs you to be "a cheerleader."

Determine how you can inspire more people to be involved in evangelism and to grow in their walk with Jesus. Implement these plans.

GOOD QUESTIONS TO ASK

1. Why does your church exist? How is it doing in accomplishing that purpose?

2. What is the vision of your new church? What difference does it make in the lives of the people who are a part of the family of faith?

3. What intentional steps are you taking to create momentum among the people within the church? What steps are you taking to generate momentum that is felt also within the community?

4. How do faith, hope and love show themselves in your life and ministry? Which of these is the biggest challenge to you? Why?

5. What values, dreams, attitudes and lifestyle do you see "reflected back" to you from the congregation? What should you attempt to change or reinforce?

6. How intentional is the evangelism and outreach aspect of your lifestyle? Who are you influencing to be more this way?

7. What is it that enables you to be an inspiring leader?

DIGGING DEEPER

Malphurs, Aubrey. *Planting Growing Churches for the 21st Century.* 2nd edition. Grand Rapids, MI: Baker Books, 1998.

Maxwell, John. *Leadership Lessons for Every Day.* Nashville, TN: J. Countryman, 2003.

Patrick, Darren. *Church Planter: The Man, the Message, the Mission.* Wheaton, IL: Crossway, 2010.

Sjogren, Steve, Ping, Dave and Pollock, Doug. *Irresistible Evangelism.* Loveland, CO: Group Publishing, 2004.

Strobel, Lee and Mittelberg, Mark. *The Unexpected Adventure.* Grand Rapids, MI: Zondervan, 2009.

2

Calling and Motivation

Pastor Joe was ready for the challenge. Three years ago while he was still in seminary, Joe had come to grips with the reality God was calling Him to plant a new church. He had not asked for this kind of assignment from God, nor did he really want it. But Joe had become convinced beyond a shadow of a doubt that this was indeed the ministry calling God had placed upon his life. Like Martin Luther years before, Joe declared he "could do no other."[15]

Pastor Joe had done what he could to prepare himself for the work ahead. He finished school and received the appropriate training. He had read all the applicable books he could find. He had even interviewed every church planter in the area. All of these things quickly taught him one thing: you couldn't give yourself to this ministry calling half-heartedly. It was a "do or die, all or nothing" kind of ministry. It would take all he had to offer, but he and his family felt they were up for the task. They believed God had shaped them for this work.

In point of fact, this reality was truer than Joe realized. God had custom-designed him for the challenge ahead of him. His personality, his abilities, his giftedness, his passions and even his experiences had prepared him for this moment in time. God had called him to plant a church, and He had gifted him to do it. This was God's calling on His life; it was his destiny. Pastor Joe was ready, with God's help, to see it happen.

Now that he was on the field, Joe knew how important unconditional surrender to God's calling on his life actually was. There had already been times when he had wanted to give up and quit (can you say, almost every day?), but his certainty of God's calling and his fierce determination to see it through had helped him in the tough times. Progress was slow—at times, very slow—but things were beginning to move forward. Success was in sight.

To be sure, a part of the American dream is to succeed. All of us want to be successful in life. Honestly, it's not just cultural conditioning; it's part of the human experience. We want our lives to count for something. This is especially true when we are younger. In our youth and young adulthood, we see the world more idealistically and our own ability with greater naïveté. Most of us think we can make a difference; some of us actually believe we can change the world. Later in life, we are more pragmatic at best, more cynical at worst. Opportunities come our way, but they involve risk. Risk is the enemy of comfort. We often remain where we find ourselves. Success gives way to something else: resignation, satisfaction or if we're lucky, significance.

It's no coincidence that most planters are young. Their idealism makes them optimistic, opportunistic risk-takers. Mark Batterson would call them "lion-chasers."[16] They are fearless and daring; undaunted and up to the challenge. No mountain is too high; no sea is too deep. They are determined and believe with all their might that they will prevail. It's inevitable. Failure is inconceivable. *"For nothing will be impossible with God"* (Luke 1:37), right?

CALLING

There are several characteristics of these planters, like Pastor Joe, which enable them to make progress toward achievement. They need to succeed. It's not just a wish or a dream; they intensely need it. And that encompasses their calling from God.

The Bible teaches all believers have a calling from their Maker (Ephesians 4:1). That calling involves several components, including first and foremost, a calling into relationship with God Himself (Matthew 11:28-30). God is invested in us knowing Him and experiencing His love in our lives. He wants us to open our lives to Him and, out of relationship, to desire to follow Him.

This calling also leads us into relationship with others who name the name of Jesus (Hebrews 10:24-25). We are called into community to model Christ's love for us to one another. This is evidently because we now all share the fatherhood of God, making us brothers and sisters in Christ. It also springs, though, from our need for genuine fellowship and community with others who complement us and brings wholeness to our life experience.

The calling of God further exhibits itself in service, one that is edifying to the Body of Christ and ministering as an agent of God's grace to those who are yet to know Him. In other words, God's calling on our lives prompts us "to do" on His behalf (Ephesians 2:10). While some of these manifestations are common to all of us as believers (e.g., testify, intercede, show generosity, etc.), other components are specialized and unique to what has traditionally been known as a "vocation" (Latin for "calling") or role in ministry. These vocations, biblically speaking, are not relegated only to professional, fulltime clergy positions. A calling from God is lived out in all fields of work and labor. The Puritans of England and early America wrote extensively on this topic.[17]

In this chapter though, our interest is upon those God has called into the roles of service within, or for, the Christian church. This calling into ministry—often known as fulltime or bi-vocational Christian service—takes a myriad of forms, from the pastorate to student ministry to work in a parachurch organization. Some church workers (for lack of a better "generalist" term) speak of their calling in a non-specific manner as "a call to ministry," "a call to church work," or even "a call to preach." Church planters rarely (did I say how rarely?) claim such a calling. An overwhelming majority is convinced God has called them to serve Him specifically in church planting (not even pastoring, which is seen as a different or much broader role).

Why is this important? Here's why: the narrow focus and understanding of this calling is what keeps them at the wheel during the most difficult of storms. They know what God has called them to do, and they are passionate about accomplishing it. It drives them to succeed. Sometimes it will be the only thing that keeps them at their duty station, but it is enough. Genuinely called church planters evidence perseverance and determination, with an overwhelming belief that God will bring them through the storm better than they were before it. They are not quitters on God or others. Come what may, their calling functions as the anchor to Jesus in their life.

> Genuinely called church planters evidence perseverance and determination, with an overwhelming belief that God will bring them through the storm better than they were before it.

PERSONALITY

My wife has a theory about church planters. She believes all the good ones have ADHD. While this theory may be exaggerated beyond its own merits, there is some truth to it, at least for those planters who are more catalytic in nature. Planters are by nature "doers." They are in constant motion, continual activity. In fact, the busyness of planters is overwhelming to those who are not planters. And while all good planters may not literally have ADHD (though it would be an interesting research project, don't you think?), it is very typical for them to be "Type A" personalities. This personality type is not "laid back" and passive in regards to life. On the contrary, they are take-charge, squeeze-every-drop-you-can-out-of-life, pro-active personalities. To say that they are driven would likely be an understatement! Their eager and aggressive assertiveness makes things happen, even as it may offend others along the way.

The problem with Type A planters is their drivenness can come from somewhere other than their calling from God. Gordon MacDonald has a great discussion of this in his classic book, *Ordering Your Private World*.[18] MacDonald reminds his readers that driven people are often not centered people. He suggests their drivenness can be prompted by a need for approval or achievement that was missing in their past. On the other hand, it can be initiated by a bad experience from which they are running.

However, not all drivenness is necessarily bad; it truly can come from one's calling and pursuit of pleasing God through His claim upon one's life. The apostle Paul is a great illustration of this reality. By all accounts, the biblical record paints him as a driven church planter. What was it that "drove" him? While I readily admit that I am not a psychologist, it seems to me that he was motivated by at least the following things: the mercy and grace of God shown Him (especially regarding his past), the love of God (which compelled him to share with others) and the "high calling of God in Christ Jesus" (which pulled him forward in ministry). These are good and noble motivations that also drive many church planters today.

Most planters are extroverts by nature, which indeed is helpful for initiating new relationships, communicating God's Word effectively, leading others in decision-making and other entrepreneurial-type enterprises necessary in starting a church from nothing. In fact, at least one research project on the topic has found that extroverted planters—according to the DiSC personality inventory—are more successful numerically with their church plants than those who are more introverted.[19] Perhaps God has hardwired their desire for greater numerical impact into the very personality makeup of their lives.

PROPER MOTIVATION

Church planters have all kinds of motivations for planting a church. The *Discovery Day Teaching Manual* suggests that among the poorest of motivations are these:

- ➢ Desire to pastor a large church
- ➢ Be the next hero or seminar leader
- ➢ Like a particular worship style or method
- ➢ Leave a bad/undesirable situation
- ➢ Everyone else is doing it

The manual, created by the North American Mission Board of the Southern Baptist Convention, goes so far as to claim these are "unhealthy" reasons for planting a church.[20]

The aforementioned motivators for the apostle Paul (the mercy and grace of God, the love of God, the calling of God), on the other hand, are among those healthy reasons, often cited by church planters. Each of these adds valuable insights to the effective church planter. The mercy and grace of God are overwhelming, when one stops long enough to reflect on them. God uses these to provide us with newness of life in Christ, a life totally undeserved or merited in any way. The mercy of God wipes out our failures and shortcomings through the blood of Christ; the grace of God gifts and shapes us for use in His Kingdom beyond our wildest imagination. Paul realized both of these realities. With God's mercy he who was once a persecutor of the church became an apostle for the church. With God's grace he who was imprisoned and physically beaten by enemies became the Almighty's voice to kings and governors. The power of forgiveness and gifted opportunity motivated Paul.

So did the love of Christ. In 2 Corinthians 5:14, he speaks of its compelling place in his life. It motivated him to share the message of reconciliation with God wherever he could, even to the point of persuasion, though others might ridicule or persecute him. It caused him to nurture and care for God's people as a mother cares for her children (1 Thessalonians 2:7). It enabled him to give freely of his life to others, because he knew it was not his own (1 Corinthians 6:20).

Then there's the high calling of God (Philippians 3:14), of which we have already written much in this chapter. Paul's experience prompts a few additional insights, though. This calling is as much about the "finish line" in ministry as the beginning. While the beginning forces us forward, the finish line calls us to completion. This calling is found in its goal: to know Christ (Philippians 3:10) and to make Him known (Romans 1:16-17). It is a calling to walk close to God throughout life and to share the life-transforming message of His Gospel with others, so that they can become His disciples, too.

All effective church planters have one or more of these motivating factors influencing their lives. It will show in their behavior and it will be heard in their conversation. It will get them up in the morning and keep them up at night. It illuminates their darkest moments and it underscores their greatest accomplishments. These motivators bring glory to God and propel planters to succeed.

SUCCESS AND FAILURE

To be sure, "success" is an elusive thing. Most people agree that success should not be defined just numerically. Such metrics are often seen as "worldly" or "egocentric." Certainly, they don't reveal the entire picture. To be sure, there is far more to success than simply numbers. However, one cannot discount the reality that numbers represent people. In fact, even the Bible makes much of numbers. Take the book of Acts for example, where time and again the record of the early church is recited to the reader in terms of numerical growth and expansion. The Old Testament even has a book called "Numbers!"

While the saying "we count numbers because numbers count," has some legitimacy to it, numbers certainly don't tell the whole story. Church planters know this and, especially in the early days, they are unwilling to allow numbers to define them or the progress they've made. In fact, they are often reticent to offer numbers for informational purposes because they fear the numbers might lead to unfair comparisons or leave much out of the comprehensive picture of what God is doing in their midst. After all, church planters are risk-takers and some of the risks they take can lead to the loss of people rather than a gain, at least in the short-term. But they risk just the same.

> "Failure" is one of the few words that a church planter removes from his dictionary.

"Failure" is one of the few words that a church planter removes from his dictionary. Because of its emotional impact and psychological weight, planters will not tolerate failure. Yet, as risk-takers they always have the potential to be unable to accomplish what they had anticipated. Many times they won't achieve the expected result. So how do they transcend the chasm of reality and refuse to give in to failure? They redefine it.

- Planters talk of failure as "unfaithfulness to the calling or the task."
- Failure means "not trying or, on the other hand, giving up."
- Failure is seen as an "unwillingness to take a chance or meet a need."
- Failure is "settling for the status quo."

Because this is so, planters intuitively know that some of the things they attempt will not accomplish the end result. However, learning that reality through experience enables them to move on and try something else that eventually, they believe, will indeed work. Real failure in the eyes of a new church starter is the refusal to try anything, at all.

When planters are willing to be trailblazers, to "go where no one has gone before," it is then that they believe the numbers—good or bad—will take care of themselves. Pragmatically they realize that the only way ever to succeed is to try, to give it your best and most noble effort, and let God take care of the growth (1 Corinthians 3:6).

DESPERATION

Over the past few years where I live, wrens have annually chosen to build a nest within our screened patio. I have watched with admiration as they fearlessly gather the materials necessary to create this place that will serve as a temporary dwelling place for their children-to-be. After they have finished and the eggs have been laid, it is interesting to observe the steps they take to protect and provide for the newly born birds. One parent will guard them from predators at the nest, while the other parent will find food to sustain them. But soon, these young fledgling birds are forced out of the nest to learn the things for which they were created, including flight and life beyond the nest on their own. Birds are born to fly, not simply to stay in the nest. Their future depends on it.

This may be the most obvious reason planters need to succeed, too: their future depends upon it. Almost every planter has a portion of his financial support (if not all of it) provided through fundraising, denominational support, partner organizations and friends who underwrite the early days of their work. Some planters have funding assistance for only a matter of months, while others may have it last for a few years. Regardless, there is always an ending point down the road, a time in which this financial aid will be no more. By that time, it is believed the church planter, through means of the new church that has been started, will be financially supported.

The organizations and partners involved are not heartless in this matter, to be sure. They know through research and experience that planters and their churches need to be shifted from financial subsidies to self-support in a short period of time. They also do not want to create a "welfare mentality" among those receiving the funding, so a deadline is set on the horizon at which time the financial assistance will cease. Planters have to prepare to "leave the nest" and embrace their future.

Planters, as one might imagine, are anxiously aware of this reality from the very beginning. They know the clock is ticking on them and their new work opportunity. And while they would eagerly accept additional money—and time—to get the church to the place where they believe self-support would be more feasible, they readily accept the challenge. Inherent within the challenge is the need to succeed or else everything they've hoped and dreamed will come to an abrupt or languishingly drawn-out end.

This "ticking clock" provides adequate incentive to most planters to be the self-starting, entrepreneurial, risk-taking leaders they of necessity must be in order to survive down the road. It leads to a sense of genuine desperation, of real and obvious abandonment to the call. Their efforts show it in a number of ways. They are judicious with their resources and use of time. They take initiative in meeting and developing relationships. They take chances where only God can provide for them, and where not surprisingly, they discover the arms of God awaiting them.

> Church planters write "No Exit" above the other possibilities in life.

Church planters write "No Exit" above the other possibilities in life. The only way to succeed is to accomplish what they have been called to do. Thus, they are passionately committed to succeed, whatever the cost. As someone has said before, "Church planters will assault hell with a water pistol, if God asks." Failure is not an option.

NEXT STEPS

APPLY TO YOUR SETTING

Reflect on your calling. Write it down; this will help you clarify it in your heart and mind. Think about the way it has been sharpened over the years. Discern the implications this may have for your ministry in the years yet to come.

Take one or more personality inventories, if you have not already done so. Analyze the results and meditate on the differences they can make in your ministry. Do this with your entire staff or team, too; you'll be glad you did.

Evaluate your drive and motivations in ministry today, where you are. Determine if they have changed and, if so, the cause of those changes. Repent of any unhealthy, worldly motives that may be discovered.

Examine your feelings and thoughts about success and failure. Determine as best you can "why you do what you do." Decide to live for an audience of only One—Almighty God Himself.

Think about your own sense of urgency and desperation in ministry; does it exist? Without being reckless, figure out how such "desperation" for God and His calling on your life should look. Adjust your behavior accordingly.

GOOD QUESTIONS TO ASK

1. What is your understanding of God's calling upon your life? How does that impact your behavior?

2. How does your personality affect your efforts as a church planter? Where is it helping you? Where is it hindering you?

3. What are the motivating factors behind your church planting experience? Why do you do what you do? Who are you trying to please?

4. How do you define success? How do you handle failure? What determines the difference between them?

5. What are the urgent things in your life for which you are passionate, even desperate, to see achieved? Why these things? What will it take to make them reality?

DIGGING DEEPER

Batterson, Mark. *In a Pit with a Lion on a Snowy Day.* Nashville, TN: Multnomah, 2006.

Guinness, Os. *The Call.* Nashville, TN: W Publishing, 2003.

McCrary, Larry, et al. *Discovery Tools.* Alpharetta, GA: North American Mission Board, SBC, 2002.

McDonald, Gordon. *Ordering Your Private World.* Nashville, TN: Thomas Nelson, 1985.

McNeil, Reggie. *A Work of Heart.* San Francisco, CA: Jossey-Bass, 2011.

3

Vision and Focus

Pastor Joe was excited about God's call upon his life. He had come to feel quite early in the process that God had a special and unique idea in mind for Redemption Fellowship. This "vision" was Joe's understanding of what God wanted to accomplish through the new church in the coming years. He felt he "knew" what God expected the church to be and he was anxiously expectant about it...in fact, he wanted to move on with seeing it become reality.

How did he come to this realization? Pastor Joe spent a lot of time in prayer, agonizing over what God's own vision was for the community. As he felt he was beginning to realize what God was seeing, the pastor also began to understand what God wanted the new church to be. The goal was to impact the lostness of the community and bring transformation to the lives of the people who lived there. It actually excited Pastor Joe so much that many nights he found it impossible to sleep! The daytime wasn't much better; he found himself lost in the dream of what he envisioned God preparing to do through him.

When Pastor Joe moved to the town where Redemption Fellowship was to be planted, he shared the difference-making "vision of transformation" with anyone and everyone he could tell. His eyes would dilate and the pace of his voice would pick up speed. He became more animated as he visually described the impact this new church was going to have upon the community. He always included details describing the change (for the better) that would be experienced by every resident in town, young or old, churched or unchurched. Jesus was going to use this new community of believers to rescue souls, save marriages and make the town a better place for everyone to live.

As the church planter shared, family by family and individual by individual would often be "caught up" in the vision of what God was going to do through Pastor Joe and Redemption Fellowship. They wanted to be a part of seeing these things happen! Because this was the case, they committed themselves to the future of the new church. For some of the early responders, this meant being sent out from partnering churches to unite with what God was doing through Redemption Fellowship. However, for most of those who wanted to join this effort, it meant committing their own lives to Christ and first following Him themselves. This required personal transformation for them individually and in addition, participation with the young community of faith in bringing their Savior to the city. They all wanted their lives to count for something; they wanted to make a difference!

Later, as individuals began to commit to the young church, the vision became a filtering mechanism in the "discovery class" required of all members. It helped the leadership of the church keep the entire community of disciples headed in the same direction. In addition, it helped Pastor Joe and his leadership to maintain their focus on what God wanted to accomplish through them. This was important, because the new church quickly discovered that it was very easy to spread itself too thin by trying to do too much. To their relief, the vision fixed their attention on what was most important, the very reason for which God had created them in the first place.

Vision is an amazing thing. Because it is expressed in picture words, vision has the ability to engage our emotions, to tug at our heart and to command our allegiance. If it is shared well, one is able to "see it," prompting us to act upon its compelling possibilities. In fact, God-given visions are not simply seen as possibilities, but rather as realities waiting to happen. It is our privilege and opportunity to join God in what He has already told us that He desires to do.

Vision, simply defined, is "a preferred future." As believers, we understand it to be God's preferred future, one He has invited us to share with Him in becoming reality. Randy, one of my colleagues, refuses to use the word "vision," eschewing it for the preferable word "revelation." He has a point. Vision, apart from God disclosing to His followers what He is about to do, is nothing more than fantasy or illusion. On the other hand, genuine vision is the stuff by which every good church planter is shaped.

PULLED FORWARD

A part of the compelling nature of vision is that it is forward-looking. While many people, and even more churches, prefer to look backward over their proverbial shoulder to the past, new churches and their leaders refuse to do so. In fact, they can't since they have no past to influence such perspective or process in their decision-making. The only way they can live is forward.

> Vision, apart from God disclosing to His followers what He is about to do, is nothing more than fantasy or illusion.

This is a distinct advantage, and one every planter acknowledges. Vision pulls you forward into the future. It is compelling and alluring. It entices and engages the senses. More importantly, it quickens the heart, providing the soul with a "difference-making" *raison d'être*. Like a magnet exhibiting its power, vision captivates the imagination. It is a powerful motivator.

Far too many churches today fail to capitalize on the "forward pull" of vision. They are seduced by the past. Previous successes can paralyze a church into inactivity or "more of the same." Routine bores the spirit and risk dies. Stepping out in faith is unwanted and fear sets in. Managing the success of the past saps the energy of a congregation and eventually stalls progress. Vision requires courage. Without it, comfort is all that matters.

Previous failures can weigh down a congregation, too, like baggage slowing down its owner. Unless it is opened and emptied, the owner has little chance of ever escaping its influence. Rather than being eagerly compelled to move into the future, failures—including, most notably, church splits or moral mistakes—angrily push a congregation wildly and recklessly into the unknown. With no boundaries or goal to guide it, failure begins a spiral downward toward compounded heartache and chaos. Vision provides clarity.

Vision from God is authoritative. It inspires faith and defines reality. Like a star on the horizon, it demands focused attention and eager awareness of its presence on every hill and deep within every valley. Without it travelers are uncertain where they are located. Vision provides a north star, a constant in an ever-changing world. Vision orients.

For a church planter, apart from the call of God there is nothing more directive, more motivating, more passionately felt than the vision God has given. It is all-encompassing, all-consuming in the early days of processing what God is seeking to do through the planter in the establishment of this new church. It is, at least metaphorically, "everything."

STEWARDSHIP OF VISION

Vision is a gift from God. It is certainly undeserved, but God in His infinite wisdom and plan has determined for human beings like you and me to join Him in what He is seeking to accomplish on this earth. While He "owns" the vision, He shares it with His people, typically through chosen (i.e., called out for this specific purpose) servants. As recipients of this revelation, these servants become stewards of it. The privilege and blessing of God's grace demand their responsibility and obedience.

> This is one of the more telling distinctions found in all church planters with growing congregations: they have others who own the vision with them.

In other words, church planters are not just recipients of this vision. They are obligated to share it with others, who will make it their stewardship, as well. Effective church planters are able to empower others to see and understand the vision and to desire to submit themselves, under God, to its direction upon their lives. In fact, this is one of the more telling distinctions found in all church planters with growing congregations: they have others who own the vision with them. Certainly, no one other than the planter can of necessity be the guardian of the vision or the primary vision-caster in the new church. However, these additional leaders have so owned the vision that they are able to describe it in ways that capture the hearts of other individuals and families, so that they too want to join the cadre of people who live to see the vision become reality.

Church planters receive the vision; they cast the vision in ways that cause others to want to own it with them. They also implement the vision. They recognize that knowing the vision is never enough. Stewardship requires that they do everything within their power to allow God to use them to turn the dream into reality. They long for the day when they reach the horizon God has shown them and are able to celebrate God's goodness...only to long for Him to reveal to them the next "preferred future" He has for them ahead.

Planters who don't have a sense of God's vision or who find themselves unable to communicate God's vision will ultimately be unable to get the new church off the ground. Force of personality alone won't get them very far. Polished communication skills will only enamor people for so long. In addition, if they are unable to unify people around the vision and effectively get them to begin to implement a process to achieve the vision, then people will begin to disengage and withdraw from participation. Vision kindles the desire in people to make their lives count for something; over time, if no progress is apparent toward that "something," then many will leave. Unfulfilled vision frustrates.

SINGLE-MINDEDNESS

When God revealed His vision to my wife Joye and me for the first church we together joined Him in planting, we were living in southern California. Though we were three thousand miles away, God burdened us for the people of metropolitan Boston, Massachusetts. We began to "see" the things we believed God wanted to do through us, so we actively prepared ourselves for what was to come. We prayed and planned. We researched and reached out to others who knew planting and/or the area. And when we were certain that this was God's preferred future for us, we closed the door on the direction in life we'd been pursuing in lieu of God's vision ahead.

From that moment on, nothing was going to distract us from the vision God had set before us. So, we packed up the few things we owned and together with our eighteen-month old daughter, Sarah, we moved coast to coast to a place we'd never lived, all because we were certain of God's calling and vision for our lives.

Church planters will sacrifice just about anything for the sake of the vision. Like us, they will uproot their family and travel to a remote spot in the world because of it. They will give up a nice salary for it. They will forsake benefits to make it come true. Planters will turn their back on comfort and conveniences, because they believe this vision is a specific and personal privilege they have been given. It is an individual and special opportunity to partner with God in something they feel He has created them uniquely to accomplish.

Because of this, the Enemy will do everything within his power to distract them from the vision. Some of his subtle temptations include:

- Substituting another ministry for God's call to plant a church
- Focusing on churched people rather than the lost
- Adding programs and activities that keep people busy, though these things have nothing to do with the vision

- Intimidating them by way of distracted looks at the ministries of other church leaders and their congregations
- "Turfism" by other churches
- Denominational "aerobics" that keep them from the vision
- Isolation
- Pastoral care at the expense of evangelism and outreach

Some of these things are not bad or "wrong," in and of themselves. And there are obviously many more temptations, as well. Often, though, these are used to tempt a servant of God to settle for the good, rather than the best. They are attempts to distract the planter from the specific purpose God has for him to accomplish.

Planters may be surprised by the attacks and distractions early in their ministry, especially when they come from well-intentioned church or denominational leaders. Their naïveté can allow others to take advantage of what appears from the outside to look like a lack of activity. Filling in for others here or challenging the planter to relocate there can be confusing, discouraging and debilitating. Don't they understand the calling and vision God has given?

Actually, they don't, unless the planter has drawn the proverbial line in the sand. Others are simply trying to fulfill their calling to the best of their ability, too. Effective planters come to understand this and set boundaries around their own ministry calling and vision. Then, like racehorses headed toward the finish line, they put on blinders to keep themselves from being distracted. Their single-mindedness is all about the vision. Like a zealot passionately pursuing a life-or-death cause, they adamantly and obsessively refuse to let anything get in their way.

Their calling prompts their passion. Their passion fuels their focus. Their focus advances the vision.

SIMPLE CHURCH

In 2006 Thom Rainer and Eric Geiger wrote a book entitled *Simple Church*. In the short years that have passed since it was published, it has already become the best selling ministry book by Broadman & Holman of all time. The book (not to be confused with the "simple/organic/house church" concept) argues that the congestion of church activity can diminish the effectiveness of the church as a whole. A simpler approach is needed. Even more important, a clearer understanding of the church's objective is necessary for the Body of Christ to accomplish its God-ordained assignment.[21]

Churches need to apply the wisdom of *Simple Church* to their own ministry. All of us have the same amount of time. We can only do so much. Attempting to do more will leave things undone, promote mediocrity or produce burnout. There are really no exceptions to this rule. The only way around it is to find more people, who will in turn apply their own time to the efforts at hand. But even that adds complexity to the corporate life of the living Church. And complexity eventually slows growth in all living organisms.

New churches have an advantage here. They realize (obviously!) that they can't do everything; it would be ridiculous to try. As a result, they stay focused on the necessary elements in accomplishing the assignment God has given them: to fulfill His vision for this new church. They streamline and simplify. They eliminate whatever is unnecessary and unneeded. They don't worry about what the church down the street is doing. Instead, they stay true to their calling. They effectively represent God in their community through the dream He originally used to capture their hearts.

> **Simple church results in a growing church.**

Simple church results in a growing church.

WARNING! DANGER AHEAD

We have had three teenage children grow up in our home, Sarah, Jonathan and Rebekah. Each is unique and special in his or her own way. Each is skilled and talented, smart and thrilling to be around (most of the time). Joye and I marvel at their maturity and enjoy their insights. We have learned much from them, as they have grown older.

However, we are thankful that they are leaving the teenage years behind. The years had moments that were excruciatingly painful and agonizingly difficult. The children were, like Joye and I before them, brooding and withdrawn at times, erratic and inconsistent, and struggling to find focus in life. We learned through this time that growing older is not the same thing as growing up.

I would love to tell you that new churches stay focused, that they continue to grow up effectively as they get older. Unfortunately, I can't do that. In fact, by year four their evangelistic conversion growth rate, even if it was tremendous in the early years, begins to decline. In some cases the decline is rather dramatic. In fact, if the new church is made up of transfer growth from the parent church or other churches in town (or worse, from disgruntled former church members, often called the "dechurched" in literature today), the transition may happen even quicker. A church like this "prematurely ages," since it carries with it the DNA of long-established churches.

This decline is the result of another subtle temptation with which the Enemy tantalizes new churches: become a "full service" church.

Have something for everyone who enters your doors.
Meet every need.
Do all you can.

It's a temptation I see confront every church planter. It is one that tempted me, as well.

Effective church planters don't abandon the vision God has given them for the vision of another. They refuse to clone a nationally-known leader's vision in place of God's own vision for their work. They are unwilling to create a compilation of all visions for the one vision God has chosen for them.

They stay narrowly focused, with steely determination and firm boundaries on what should be done now, and what should not. To enlarge and broaden the effort too soon only weakens the foundation. Vision demands strength.

NEXT STEPS

APPLY TO YOUR SETTING

Examine your vision statement. (If you don't have one, create one under God's leadership.) Analyze how it is impacting the behavior of the people in the congregation.

Look at your organization's systems and processes. Determine if they are all connected to, and grow out of, the vision. Anticipate the outcomes they will produce.

Evaluate how the vision is shared and implemented in your church. Assess your stewardship of it with those who lead and can make a difference. Remember, vision "leaks" and needs to be re-shared regularly, maybe even once a month, in some way.[22]

Determine the focus level of your new church. Cut away any excess programs and activities that keep you from staying single-minded and ruthless when it comes to the vision.

GOOD QUESTIONS TO ASK

1. What is God's vision for your new church? Who else needs to know this?

2. What is your role in handling the vision God has given you: discoverer, sharer, implementer, guardian? What's keeping you from being your best in that role?

3. How is the vision getting to the people? What means are being used?

4. What temptations are attempting to distract you from the vision God has given? What are you going to do about these distractions?

5. What is your church doing now that it needs to stop doing, in order to stay focused on the vision? What about you personally? How will you go about making these changes?

DIGGING DEEPER

Barna, George. *Turning Vision into Action.* Ventura, CA: Regal Books, 1996.

McNeal, Reggie. *Practicing Greatness.* San Francisco, CA: Jossey-Bass, 2006.

Rainer, Thomas and Geiger, Eric. *Simple Church.* Nashville, TN: Broadman & Holman Publishing, 2008.

Stanley, Andy. *Visioneering.* Sisters, OR: Multnomah Publishers, 1999.

4

Passion for Those without Jesus

Pastor Joe had a recurring dream. In his dream, he was standing on the deck of a cruise ship moving through the ocean. As the big ship sped through the waters, he became aware of people, hundreds and thousands of nameless people in the water bobbing up and down as they cried out for help. This was life and death to them!

In Joe's dream, he anxiously tried to figure out what to do. He thought about jumping in but realized he could only save one at a time. He thought about the life preserver, but even with that he came to the same realization. Instead, in his dream, he released small boats from onboard the ship into the water and these were able to carry many drowning people to safety.[23]

Joe likened his dream to the impulse he felt for the lost all around him. It was a burden that bothered him all the time. More than bothered him, it motivated him to live his life in such a way that the priority of his ministry was focused on those without Jesus. He planned his day with the intentional expectation that he would have chances to share Christ's love with those who need to know it. He chose to hang out in places where he intersected the lives of those without Jesus. Joe knew from personal experience how much they mattered to God, because someone had made the effort to make sure he knew that, too, once upon a time.

At Redemption Fellowship, Joe reminded the people of William Temple's statement years ago, "The church is the only institution that does not exist for itself."[24] He would constantly lobby the leadership for consideration of the "silent participants," as he called them, those lost and yet unreached people in our community. Joe felt that if someone didn't speak up for them—their needs, concerns, perspective, etc.—then they would too easily be forgotten.

Because of this, Pastor Joe made sure the church planned with the unreached in the forefront of their mind. Efforts would be made to "get outside" the building, if it would reach others. Requirements for participation were kept to a minimum, wherever possible. The environment was kept comfortable and safe for even those who had never darkened the door of a church building.

Joe knew that two "hang ups" the lost and unchurched have with the churched population are these: the need for a biblical message relevant to the life they live in the twenty-first century and a church community where there is no disconnect from that message, where the church is authentic, genuine and real. He was determined to see that Redemption Fellowship was that kind of church with that kind of message.

Effective church planting is about reaching the lost and unchurched with the Gospel of Jesus Christ. Ineffective church planting, which simply "moves sheep from one sheep pen to another" and is not focused on reaching the lost, is not really church planting at all. All legitimate church planting is evangelistic in nature and purpose.

Some might see this as an over-exaggeration, but regardless, the point should remain clear: the best of church planting is focused on reaching the lost for Jesus. The thesis of this book is built around the reality that church plants are "more effective" at evangelism than established churches. This is based on a number of research reports over the last two or three decades that validate such a conclusion. In fact, church plants are typically three times more effective than established churches in reaching the lost with the Gospel of Jesus Christ.

Thom Rainer, President of LifeWay Christian Resources, shared in a meeting with regional denominational leaders within the Southern Baptist Convention late in 2007 that the discrepancy between new churches and established churches in the area of evangelism is actually even greater than typically thought. The Annual Church Profile, a tabulated statistical report of participating SBC churches, suggested a ratio of one new person reached for every forty-five members in the average Southern Baptist church in 2006. He went on to say that the statistic is misleading, for when you remove the "re-baptisms" and the baptisms of children of church members, then the number is closer to one lost person reached for every ninety members in the church. (Baptists don't believe in a theology of "re-baptism;" rather, Rainer is referring to individuals who come to the conclusion later in life they weren't scripturally baptized previously.) Such a number is staggering, if indeed true.[25]

While this entire book is about why church plants grow so effectively, a key part of that is their evangelistic impact. This impact is found first in the heart of the church planter, who makes it a personal priority, and then in the corporate heart of the congregation as a whole. Evangelistic church plants don't just reach the lost; they are passionate about reaching the lost.

LOST PEOPLE MATTER TO THEM

The burden for lost people and their eternal destiny are a constant concern for these churches and their planting leader. They know many lost people by name. They engage them in relationship and activity. They passionately pray for their salvation. The heartache they feel for these people without Jesus moves them to action. Heartache gives way to shoe leather.

Why? In the words Bill Hybels made so famous, "Lost people matter to God."[26] As a result, the love for God these planters and their congregations feel "compels them" to care and to share the Good News whenever, wherever, however they can with those who need Jesus. For many, taking the Gospel to the ones without Jesus is THE reason why they exist at all. Consequently, it affects everything they do.

A year or two ago, a well-known American atheist, Penn Gillette of "Penn & Teller" fame, posted a YouTube video, in which he tells about his experience in receiving a copy of the Bible from an audience member at one of his shows in Las Vegas. Gillette was impressed by this man's attitude and demeanor, along with a note he had written inside the cover of the Bible he received. Though Gillette did not profess a change in his "faith status" as a result of this experience, he shared a deeply moving insight on the experience regarding the evangelistic passion, or lack thereof, that challenges all of us as believers. His conclusion to this encounter was that if we believe the claims of the Gospel to be true and eternity truly hangs in the balance for those without Jesus, "How much do you have to hate somebody to believe that everlasting life is possible, and not tell them that?"[27]

> "How much do you have to hate somebody to believe that everlasting life is possible, and not tell them that?"

Effective church planters eat, sleep and live for the lost; each person without Jesus matters to them, because they matter to God. They are constantly restless and eager to engage others who need to know of Jesus, too. They carry His burden into their mission field.

This changes the way they live their life. They intentionally frequent places where they know the lost will gather. They travel to parks, the beach, civic meetings, school gatherings and social events, all in hopes of getting to know others and building relationships with ones who need Jesus. Those who are more daring will even regularly visit bars, racetracks, certain street corners or casinos, because they know they'll encounter people without Jesus there. They are convinced Jesus would do the same, if He were walking upon the earth today.

Not only are their thoughts and schedules impacted by the concern they have for the lost, their family life is, too. They will typically open their homes to lost neighbors for dinner or coffee. They will participate or start neighborhood watch groups. Children of planters will join community recreation leagues, where both they and their parents have opportunities to get to know others who don't yet know Jesus and His love for them.

Life for effective church planters is intentional, deliberate and highly evangelistic, motivated by a love for the lost they see all around them.

ADVOCACY

In the earliest days of most church plants there are few, if any, people committed to the on-going viability of the new church beyond the planter's own family. Because this is the norm, the planter's thoughts and actions are naturally inclined to those who are still "unreached." Of course, over time people will become a part of the church, reached with the Gospel and/or joining because they desire to be a part of what God's doing through the new church. At this point in the life of almost every new church, the "gravity" of the ministry begins to shift inward; many voices already within the church family cry out for additional attention and time. The most effective church planters don't sacrifice the needs of those lost around them for the needs of the sheep already safely within the sheepfold. They find other ways to address internal needs while keeping the focus on those without Jesus.

To that end, especially when they are in meetings with staff, teams or even the whole congregation, these planters will "speak" for the lost who are not present in the congregation...yet. This is a key element in their thinking, that one day in the future God will give them a chance to see these individuals enter into relationship with Him. They believe it and thus, it compels such planters to voice needs, concerns and objections for those who are unable to advocate for themselves. They remind other leaders in the church this is

> **The most effective church planters don't sacrifice the needs of those lost around them for the needs of the sheep already safely within the sheepfold.**

why the church exists and that all people who have found redemption, including each of them, were at one point just as those outside of relationship with Christ currently are.

Advocacy never forgets the roles of grace and mercy in the life of individuals, families and even communities. It takes seriously the intercessory role we have before God on their behalf; it also takes seriously the privilege of *"paraceleo,"* the ministry of walking alongside others in their most difficult and unlovely times of life. It defends not their sin, but the sinner; it protects not their wrong, but what could become right. It loves beyond their fault and embraces their need. It elevates their worth to a "God perspective" rather than a worldly view. In some small way, it enables us to partner with the Holy Spirit, who is the ultimate Advocate and Paraclete, as He speaks into their lives with His convicting and comforting power.

This is ultimately one of the reasons why churches, especially new ones, are committed to multiplication at the congregational level. When I was leading our new church to plant other churches in metropolitan Boston, Massachusetts, we realized quickly that the culture of New Englanders was suspicious of churches that were considered too large. (Ironically, their opinion of "large" equated churches of approximately three hundred or more in attendance.) In such a context, our own church plant was still determined to reach as many lost people as we could, even if they would never come to our community of faith. As a result, we developed a strategy to start a network of churches around "the Hub" of Boston, all typically small—one hundred or less—but capable of reaching more lost and unchurched people than we could ever reach by ourselves. The church plant in Winthrop, led by Church Planter/Pastor Dick May, reached over fifty in their first year alone! These people would never have come to the South Shore of Boston to join our church plant; yet, through reproducing and parenting new churches we were able to extend our advocacy for the lost to other places.

If the church is not an advocate for the lost, then it has become self-centered as a congregation and as leaders, concerned only with themselves at the expense of others. If leaders forget this is why the church exists, then believers will quickly lapse into some form of personal, and also corporate, indulgence. It is only a short step from here to becoming judgmental and to accusing or blaming others for the wrongs they commit. However, this short step is a long way from the heart of Christ, who came *"to seek and to save the lost"* (Luke 19:10).

Effective church planters and their churches never, never, never forget this. They are mindful of the fact that, save for the grace of God on their own lives, they'd be exactly as the lost now are. As a result, they are motivated to speak up for those without Jesus at all costs, even when it's not the comfortable or cool thing to do. They care more about people and eternity than self and temporal sufficiency.

PLANNING WITH THEM IN MIND

When a church planter and his church begin to advocate for the lost and give voice for them, then the church will begin to plan with the lost in mind. They will look at their budget and their schedule and make adjustments to their corporate way of living, in order to address the needs and questions of those they are seeking to reach.

With Bill Hybels and Willow Creek Community Church, a primary way this happened was through their weekend gatherings. They deliberately and intentionally planned for these experiences to be evangelistic encounters with God for the lost and unchurched, rather than worship experiences for the committed and faithful. Actual worship experiences for the churched were moved to midweek, when the committed would still come. Weekend services were used for these evangelistic encounters because they were convinced the weekend was the opportune time the lost and unchurched would even consider "going to church." So, over the years they have consistently planned the music, the message, the multimedia or dramatic elements, and even the offering time, with the unchurched in mind. Everything has been filtered through how they believe the lost would receive or react to what they experience.[28]

With Rick Warren and Saddleback, another way this happened was in the initial survey of the community that helped them shape the focus of the church and its ministry. Warren asked people to share with him the top needs in the community. Compiling the data enabled him to address these concerns in a letter he mailed to the community in which he stated that Saddleback would exist to speak to such needs and concerns. These men and their churches recognized the "felt needs" of their lost community and planned with these things in mind.[29]

Opponents will sometimes argue that this waters down or compromises the Gospel in some way. They claim it cheapens the work of Jesus on the cross. But effective planters would argue that instead it builds a bridge to the lost and enables the Gospel to gain a hearing among those who need it most. They are mindful of the apostle Paul's teaching, *"I have become all things to all people, so that I may by every possible means save some"* (1 Corinthians 9:22). These strategies, and many others, are ways in which they seek to make this bridge accessible and easy to travel.

Planters are aware that the lost often see many obstacles in the path to God. Some are intellectual, but some are experiential. Unfortunately, some of these experiential obstacles have to do with "the church" and how it represents itself before a lost and dying world. Many of the lost feel the church is judgmental, hypocritical and self-righteous. Others have had a bad experience in earlier life or in the life of a loved one. Effective planters are determined that this kind of experience will not happen in the new church they are starting, and set out to show the lost that "church" doesn't have to be "that" way.

All of this may sound harsh, especially if your church is an established church. Certainly not all churches are this way, to be sure. Unfortunately, though, many are, and these are the churches that often make the news. So when an unchurched or lost person "hears" about a church, it is often only the negative, news-making ones of which they hear. Whether or not the news is true, it doesn't encourage them to come and experience God's Good News.

New churches start because they have the lost on their collective heart, and everything they do is planned so that no other barrier, except the cross of Jesus Christ, stands in the way of the lost coming to know the Lord personally.

RELEVANCE

The *Alpha* course has been one of the most effective evangelistic tools in the history of England. *Alpha* is an evangelistic strategy developed by Pastor Nicky Gumbel at Holy Trinity Brompton Church in London. He has since taught the material in conferences and printed it in books that now traverse the globe. The strategy attempts to address intellectual objections to Christ and Christianity first, a kind of apologetics, in small group settings. Transitioning at a spiritual retreat, it presents an experiential opportunity for individuals who have moved past their intellectual concerns to encounter Christ personally. It has been wildly successful, especially among educated people groups.[30]

While the evangelistic efforts of *Alpha* have done extremely well, membership in England's churches is still declining.[31] Unfortunately, there may be a "disconnect" in England between the experiences of those converted through courses like *Alpha* and the churches they choose to visit. This perception of a lack of relevance in the local church to the lives people live daily, right or wrong, makes the difference for literally tens of thousands of individuals. It causes many to believe Jesus offers something for them in this day and age, yet at the same time to believe the church is archaic and outdated, not where their needs will be met.

> The church of the twenty-first century has to reclaim the relevance of the early church.

The church of the twenty-first century has to reclaim the relevance of the early church.

Planters and their accompanying leaders in growing churches are determined to demonstrate that the church connects with life as we live it today. They operate under the assumption that the Word of God speaks to our needs and circumstances; they believe that Jesus is immensely practical and applicable to ALL of the concerns and situations of life. From the very beginning, they set out to show the reality of this relevance to everyone they encounter, so that others can experience the difference Jesus brings to life every day. Relevance, they are convinced, is one of the driving values in the world today.

When Christ is shown to be relevant and applicable to the various facets and domains of life, people will slow down and consider the claims He makes. They will suspend their objections and concerns long enough to listen to their heart, a heart that reminds them constantly that there's something more, something this world cannot offer. It is a spiritual need, a hunger that can only be satisfied by Jesus…a relevant Jesus, experienced in a relevant church, committed to showing the lost and unchurched the difference that Jesus alone can make.

NEXT STEPS

APPLY TO YOUR SETTING

Find ways to measure the evangelistic impact of your new church. Based on your results, determine what you can do to enable it to be more effective.

Rate your new church's advocacy for lost people who are not yet a part of your church on a scale of one to ten, with ten being the highest. Decide on one or two things that need to be done to increase the advocacy on their behalf.

Examine your worship experience and other elements of church life. Analyze the "connect" value lost and unchurched people would experience, if they came to your church. Make adjustments as needed.

Explore the relevance of your church's message, ministries and even reputation with the lost in your community. Interview those who will let you to determine if you are answering the questions they are asking.

GOOD QUESTIONS TO ASK

1. *What are the passions that move you to action in ministry? Why these specific things?*

2. *How does the evangelistic imperative of Acts 1:8 affect the way you live out your life daily? The life of your new church?*

3. *How do you address the growing leadership tension between those who have been reached and are now a part of the new church and those who are lost and still unreached? How do you advocate for those without Jesus?*

4. *How do the lost around you affect your new church's plans and activities? What obstacles would they have to*

overcome to be a part of your church, if God so led them? What changes might you need to make?

5. *In what ways does your new church attempt to be relevant with the message of the Gospel to those you are seeking to reach? How effective have you been? How are you measuring your effectiveness?*

DIGGING DEEPER

Galloway, Dale, et al. *Making Church Relevant.* Kansas City, MO: Beacon Hill Press, 1999.

Gumbel, Nicky. *The Alpha Course Manual, 2nd edition.* London: Alpha Books, 2004.

Hunter III, George G. *The Celtic Way of Evangelism: Tenth Anniversary Edition.* Nashville, TN: Abingdon Press, 2010.

Mittelberg, Mark. *Building a Contagious Church.* Grand Rapids, MI: Zondervan Publishing House, 2000.

Richardson, Rick. *Evangelism Outside the Box.* Downers Grove, IL: InterVarsity Press, 2000.

Warren, Rick. *The Purpose Driven Church.* Grand Rapids, MI: Zondervan Publishing House, 1995.

5

Creativity and Innovation

"We can't keep doing the same things and expecting different results," Pastor Joe declared. "Someone, I think it was Einstein, declared that to be the definition of insanity!"

"Well, what do we do, then?" asked Bill, one of the leaders in the one-year old Redemption Fellowship.

"The best ideas haven't been discovered yet," the pastor replied. "We've got to try new things, be creative and innovative. If the former ways worked, then the community would be knocking down our doors by now."

Pastor Joe went on to explain to the congregation a "new wineskins" approach, that new things are more effective in reaching new people. "It helps build bridges to the community where the new church is located by providing new means, methodology or ministry to the people we are seeking to reach," he said. "The message can never change, but our methods must!"

To do that, Pastor Joe looked to two specific subsets of members in his group, those younger than twenty-five years of age, along with those on "the fringe" of the new congregation. Both subsets in the congregation, he thought, afforded the church valuable insights into the ways to connect better with those in the community. These late teenagers and twenty-somethings felt the pulse of new patterns and forms in the world today and were willing to be creative and think "outside the box." In fact, most of them didn't like "the box" very much, at all.

In addition, those on the fringe of the new church had the advantage of perspective, seeing things in a different way from those who had been inside the circle for a while. "Not knowing 'the way things are done around here' will help us see opportunities—

and potential obstacles—with a new and needed set of eyes," Pastor Joe thought. *"The insights they share will help us keep things creative and fresh, and that will afford us the chance to speak into the lives of those who need Jesus," he surmised. "The day in-vention gives in to con-vention is the day we begin to die."*

In the mid-1990s I was invited to speak at a national state leadership summit within my denomination in Birmingham, Alabama. At that time, Charles Chaney was leading what was known as the "Church Extension Division," which encompassed the church planting efforts of our domestic mission board. The entire mission board—not just the church planting section—was convinced what the majority of our established churches within the denomination needed was to move beyond the rut of "This is what we've always done" to "Let's try something new." The *Start Something New* emphasis was an attempt to remind church leaders new people respond best to new initiatives. And to make the point, who did the mission board decide to bring in to speak to these leaders? None other than church planters, including me, who illustrated the power of "something new" in reaching out to a community that needs Jesus.

One of the more evident things that distinguish a new church plant from an established church is its desire to "do things differently." This out-of-the-box attitude is born out of a variety of motivations and concerns. For one thing, church planters are acutely aware that most churches fall into a routine over time. They do the same things over and over, often because these patterns are known and familiar. Planters surmise that the best ideas are untapped because decision-makers in many churches don't think hard enough about the power of innovative ways to implement their efforts. Effective church planters also realize that unreached people would likely already be in churches if the normal methods and practices used were effective in connecting with those outside of regular church life. They believe that something different has to be done, in order to gain the interest and involvement of those not yet reached.

To be honest, not all their motivations are this altruistic. Some are personal and somewhat selfish. For example, some planters have had bad experiences of their own in church life, ranging from conflict to boredom and through their church planting efforts, they desire to keep others from experiencing the same. Others personally prefer a methodology not employed in churches where they've served in the past, and because newer methods and styles resonate with them, they desire to create a community where they "like" the way church is lived out before the world. Other motivations are purer and nobler that draw most into church planting, as we have already noted in this book.

Yet, while motivations are varied, this principle applies across the board: effective church planters and the churches they lead are willing to do new things in ways that are creative and innovative, different from the way the typical established church operates in the Western world today. They are willing to take chances, to "look different," to be "edgy," etc., not just to attract attention and certainly not to be controversial; they are attempting to gain the attention of those who have not yet heard the Gospel message.

> **Effective church planters and the churches they lead are willing to do new things in ways that are creative and innovative, different from the way the typical established church operates in the Western world today.**

CREATIVITY

Over the past ten years, I've had the opportunity to assess hundreds of church planting candidates and their spouses. There are many things I've noticed about the ones who are selected by God for this calling. Their personality is typically extroverted. Their spiritual gifts usually include leadership or evangelism. A wide majority of them also have entrepreneurial and artistic skills.

This realization has huge ramifications for the way they approach church life in general and the worship experience in particular. As artists, they see the world differently; it is a matter of perception, symbol and significance. They focus on meaning and seek to find myriad means of expression, knowing that the engaging of the senses—all of them, if possible—makes impact. They think in terms of emotive effect, and they typically let people interpret and process for themselves.

As a result, the church plants they lead will appear different, starting with the most evident of items. For example, they will have "creative" names. Here in my area, we have church plants named "Gallery," "The Garden Community," "365" and "EverSpring," just to name a few. The names convey a new perspective on church and life within the community of faith, to be sure; in addition, though, they also convey something of the creative side of the planter's own artistic makeup.

They will also often prefer creative locations in which to meet. Movie theaters are popular (a form of "modern" art takes place here every day of the week), but also they will meet in art galleries, pubs, and "retro" historic buildings—including church buildings—with stained glass and antiques. These places help characterize identity and shape the new community's life together.

Creativity pulls from the fringes. This is why it is so important. Conventional thought is found in the habitual thinking patterns of our mind. All of us have traveled the path that leads us to these destinations previously; thus, it is an easy solution, because it appears to be "tried and true." It's safe. It's accepted. It's normal. At least, that's what we think.

Non-conventional types rail against the norm. To them, the norm is devoid of meaning. If it's up to them, they'll let it rest in peace, while they move on to something unique, untried and often daring. It is this kind of creativity that gets them noticed and attracts people who are not interested in "what has always been."

My daughter, Sarah, is an unconventional thinker; she is an artist in the journalism world. She is always looking for a way to do what normalcy tells the world "can't" be done. She was trying to work out her final internship at a major cable television network in New York City and was told after weeks of negotiating, that the company wouldn't be able to hire her, because of the limitations of her schedule. Sarah was disappointed, but not deterred. She refused to take "no" for an answer. She went back to her point of contact with the company and began to think outside the box regarding ways those limitations could be removed and the opportunity could be regained. Her innovation and willingness to work creatively ultimately landed her the chance to work there almost twice as long as originally expected and with a more prominent role than first envisioned.

> Effective church planters...don't live scripted lives; rather, they write a new script for how life can be lived. They apply this reality to the churches they start, as well.

Effective church planters are like this, too. They don't live scripted lives; rather, they write a new script for how life can be lived. They apply this reality to the churches they start, as well. And such creativity attracts and interests others, especially those who have been unengaged by the church in the past. New wineskins are needed to reach new people. It's often just that simple.

"RIGHT-BRAINED" ACTIVITY

The reality is that most effective church planters like this are more "right-brained" than "left-brained." In right-brained dominant people, society finds its visionaries and artists of the world. These individuals display different characteristics in their lifestyle preferences that suggest the creative nature of their minds. For example, they:

- Prefer visual instructions with examples
- Like to read fantasy and mystery stories
- Prefer groups to being one-on-one
- Dream about things that will likely never happen
- Act out stories
- Become restless during long verbal explanations
- Solve problems intuitively
- Are very spontaneous and unpredictable
- Prefer rock music[32]

Much of the above explains why new churches look and feel the way they do; they are led by individuals who value these experiences in life. The more "right-brained" they are, the more radical the orientation and eventually, the expression of church and ministry will be. My point is this: innovation is a part of their nature. It is not simply something they do. This is who they are. The result is that they are able to connect with many who have written off the traditional church because of its conventional and yes, its much more typical "left-brained" approach to worship, ministry and lifestyle.

If you pause and think about it long enough, you'll begin to realize that this explains so much about church as we know it in our Western world today. Established churches often exist in a Modern world, products of the Enlightenment and inhabited by cognitives and rationals, who exhibit the characteristics of "left-brained" minds. For example, at their weekend service they follow predictable and repetitive liturgy in worship. They preach in a linear fashion, often from the Psalms, the Prophets and the Epistles. They print detailed sermon outlines, orders of worship and calendars of events. They major on education, a mental exercise.

"Contemporary" churches are more and more found in a Postmodern world, living out life together with a "right-brained" way of thinking. At their weekend services, they have unpredictable elements of worship that will change from week-to-week, which often will include the arts in some fashion. The preaching is usually topical and more narrative from the stories of the Old Testament or the Gospels in the New Testament. They will print little or nothing for the congregation. They will major on community, a more expressive exercise. These differences are not simply the result of age; rather, they are differences in perspective that are lived out by the leadership in church life, regardless of whether the leader is twenty or fifty years old.

Church planters are more likely to be "out of the box" personalities; in fact, many of them refuse to acknowledge "the box" altogether! In established churches such people are typically on the "fringe" of the decision-making process and are relegated to the margins. They are rarely valued and affirmed; often they leave because they don't feel accepted or that they belong. But within a church plant setting these same people set the pace and make innovation central to all the community of faith experiences. Thus, tradition and routine are rarely in effect, as typically understood; rather, these people breathe uniqueness into all that the church does, because it is who they are, not simply what they do. This alone makes a difference in the priority and emphasis that creativity and innovation make in their ministry.

"YOUTH-LIKE"

I grew up during the 1970s in the deep South, where my denomination was prevalent and the opportunities for connecting with other believers my age were relatively easy. Every year at least once or twice, the youth of all of our churches in the given area would get together for what we called at the time a "youth rally." The primary experience of this youth rally-opportunity was "creative worship." At least, that's what we called it. Each creative worship "service" has distinct elements to it, including drama, contemporary (for that time) Christian music, casual dress and a speaker who was young and spoke without the need for a pulpit or lectern. There was always a significant evangelistic appeal, and as a result, many teenagers would make decisions at these rallies for Christ. The services were cool and kept students like me connected to the Body of Christ, for we sensed at times like these that the church was relevant even to us and honestly, was more than just what we saw on a typical Sunday morning within our home church.

Less than ten years later, Bill Hybels—a former youth pastor himself—launched Willow Creek Community Church in South Barrington, Illinois, following what appeared to me at the time to be a "youth rally"–type creative worship experience (after all, about 250 people from his Son City youth group became the nucleus for this new church).[33] He changed the "what" of worship to include contemporary music regularly (sometimes even Top 40 music, if the message was appropriate), open-ended drama that presented the theme of the day and a message that was practical and relevant to the world in which we live. Most importantly, its purpose was evangelistic, and those who attended were encouraged to bring their unsaved friends and neighbors with them regularly.

All of this parroted what I, and other Boomers like me, had seen and experienced in the "youth rallies" of our adolescence, but in an even better way. And it worked. Multitudes of people came to check it out; it connected with them through a new, fresh approach. Planters emerged across North America who took this paradigm and adapted it in unique and culturally-relevant ways, in order to reach the people without Jesus everywhere around them. Now, three decades later, effective planters continue to innovate with the worship experience in ways that amplify their creativity and build connections to their own community. Since many of these effective planters have previous experience in student ministry, they are tapping the lessons and methods used there to reach the younger generations not-so-far removed from those years of life themselves.

> **Effective planters continue to innovate with the worship experience in ways that amplify their creativity and build connections to their own community.**

It makes sense: build on what you know and what works.

BRIDGES AND BARRIERS

It may appear that such an approach is filled with "gimmicks" and "tricks" to entice people to attend these worship experiences. "The Gospel ought to be enough" is the objection often heard of those not doing such things. Indeed, the Gospel is enough! However, there are barriers that must be overcome before individuals in our world today are ever able to hear the gospel message at all. George Hunter, in his book *How to Reach Secular People*, suggests there are three barriers that all unchurched people have to overcome on the path to Jesus. These barriers are image, culture and the Gospel itself.[34]

Church planters and leaders need to do all they can to lower the first two of these barriers. With the first barrier, church planters have the advantage of creating an image from the start, an impossible thing for established churches to do. Planters have to overcome ignorance about their new church; they do so through positive impact on the community and through relationship-building. They seek to build upon the bridges of a winsome Gospel witness and the practical nature of following Jesus, here and now, through the lives that they live.

> The only barrier that cannot be lowered is that of the Gospel itself.

With culture, new churches attempt to make outsiders feel like insiders. They don't hold secret meetings or activities that the unchurched can't attend. They allow them to participate in leadership as openly as they feel possible. They tend to have minimal traditions and processes that "everyone here knows," but newcomers would not. They seek to build a bridge of communication that speaks plainly and clearly about God, His message of life and the relevancy of the Gospel. They refuse to speak "churchese" or use insider language that would make an unchurched person feel uncomfortable or awkward. They attempt to build an inclusive culture that others can engage and help create, if they so choose.

The only barrier that cannot be lowered is that of the Gospel itself. The Bible even tells us that the Gospel of the cross will be offensive to some (1 Corinthians 1:23). Even so, we are to share the Gospel clearly, though we cannot remove the reality of the cross for anyone. It is the only way to God.

Perceptive planters will recognize the barriers hindering those they are seeking to reach. They will creatively attempt to build bridges that transcend the barriers whenever possible. The goal is not to be the hippest or coolest "show" in town. In pragmatic terms, these planters just want to demonstrate the practical and relevant nature of the Gospel to the lives people live every day. They recognize that new means and methods are needed to connect the unchurched to the life-giving message of the Gospel. So they use them; they create them. They are convinced that if they can simply get others beyond the obstacles that keep them from "seeing" the Gospel itself, then the power of that same Gospel and the God who made it possible will do all the rest.

NEXT STEPS

APPLY TO YOUR SETTING

Evaluate the forms and methods you use in all areas of church life, especially worship. Determine whether or not artistics as well as cognitives are engaged in the programs and processes you now have in place. Adjust accordingly.

Try something new. Freshness breeds new life into a congregation. Be creative. If need be, suggest to the people that this is an ongoing "experiment" or "pilot project" that will be re-evaluated later.

Analyze the people who are a part of your church. Note those who are in their late teens and early twenties, as well as those on the fringe of church life. Ask them for ideas on what they see and experience that could be done differently.

Determine what barriers, if any, outsiders must overcome at your church to be confronted clearly by the Gospel itself. Work to remove, or at least lower, those barriers.

GOOD QUESTIONS TO ASK

1. Who are the creative, "right-brained" people in our church? What are we learning from them about how to do church effectively?

2. Who is on the "fringe" in our church, often with a contrary opinion or idea? What could we learn from them?

3. How do our youth feel about our worship experience and church, in general? Why? What lessons should we learn from them?

4. What new initiative should we add to church life for us to fulfill our purpose/vision and reach others for Jesus more effectively?

5. What feedback are we receiving about barriers others feel when considering our church? How are we addressing these issues?

DIGGING DEEPER

Gladwell, Malcolm. *Outliers.* New York, NY: Little, Brown and Company, 2008.

Hunter III, George G. *How to Reach Secular People.* Nashville, TN: Abingdon Press, 1992.

Hybels, Bill and Lynne. *Rediscovering Church.* Grand Rapids, MI: Zondervan Publishing, 1997.

Lewis, Robert. *The Church of Irresistible Influence.* Grand Rapids, MI: Zondervan Publishing, 2001.

Towns, Elmer, Stetzer, Ed and Bird, Warren. *Eleven Innovations in the Local Church.* Ventura, CA: Gospel Light, 2007.

The Power of Relationships

Pastor Joe was a busy man. He had moved to the field three months after graduating from seminary. While it might have looked to an outsider like nothing was happening, in fact the church starter was putting down deep roots and cultivating the spiritual soil in the town. He would traverse the town daily, praying as he went, and stopping frequently in the spots where he had determined the locals socially "hang out." He knew how important it was for him to build relationships with the people of the community; there was nothing he could do that would replace its impact. The reality that he had grown up in this town and was known by a number of people certainly didn't hurt his efforts to deepen and widen his circle of friends.

Beth, the pastor's wife, understood this, too. As a result, she would invite the neighbors' wives over for coffee regularly, where she had a chance to get to know them better and to practice the spiritual gift of hospitality God had given her. She would also take their infant son in his stroller down to the park daily, where she and some of the ladies caught up on life and what was happening in the community. Beth also knew that, as an outsider to the community, she had to try harder to earn the right to make an impact on the community. Credibility was built through relationship.

Together, Joe and Beth would often buy a couple of extra tickets to the movies or a concert, in order to invite another couple to join them for one of these events. They would use these opportunities as they traveled together or stopped at a coffee shop afterward to get to know the other couple better. On Fridays every week they would also invite friends and neighbors over for dinner.

They saw people relax and lower their defenses over a great, home-cooked meal. The food and fellowship enabled them to connect with these couples about family, the town, and yes, even spiritual matters like Jesus and the new church they were starting. Relationship afforded them the right to speak into another's life about the Good News of Jesus Christ.

Pastor Joe had come to realize that one of the great advantages every new church has within its grasp is the power of relationships. He wasn't about to neglect the impact he could have or the catalytic effect such relationships could bring. He knew its currency was irreplaceable by any other item of value the church—or the world, for that matter—had to offer. God had created people for relationships, and he wasn't going to let the busyness or consumerism of life crowd out the deep need every person has for "community" in his or her soul.

Pastor Joe has discovered one of the great realities of the new and fledgling church: relationships are the lifeblood of its existence. More than that, these connections with others are the powerful force that extends ownership of the new congregation to others beyond themselves. This helps build momentum and fuels the life of the new church as it grows. In this day and age, younger adults hold the value of "community" in very high esteem. People, whose lives are isolated and cloistered away more and more by the technology and automation of life, desperately need a sense of community. "Community," a word made from two other words—"common" and "unity"—affords them the opportunity to feel connected to something bigger than self (a real need that this author feels God has placed in all our hearts) and to others who are pursuing the same difference-making experience.

Because of this, community bears with it a sense of belonging for every individual whose life is touched. In fact, true community would result in more than just a life being "touched;" real community would begin the journey toward transformation for those who experience it.

The power of relationships exponentially reshapes life and an understanding of its meaning.

The more satisfying our relationships, the more impact they have on us personally and consequently, the more influence they bear on what our lives mean for others. There is nothing else a church leader can do that will bear more fruit in the future than tap into the strength of relationships.

PEOPLE MORE THAN PROGRAMS

Point of Grace, a contemporary Christian singing group, has a song on one of their earlier albums entitled, *"More than Anything,"*[35] which reminds listeners that the most important thing in creation to God is people. So simple and so obvious in its truth, this has, however, become one of the more forgotten realities in the life of many churches, especially those plateaued or declining in size. Churches, as they grow, have a need to organize and structure to handle that very growth. This is true of all living organisms, and the church is no exception. We will return to the structure issue later, but for now it is probably best simply to say that one of the steps most churches take in developing structure is to add programming to the way they live life together (i.e., community).

Programs are not bad, in and of themselves. They have received bad reviews over the past generation as a result of the anti-program bias of the younger generation. When used, though, here's the key: they must be a means to an end, not the end itself. So, in the current discussion then, attending Sunday School is not the goal; life transformation through God and His Word, experienced in community with others, is. Sunday School is only the vehicle to get people there.

Somewhere along the way many churches, especially non-growing ones, have forgotten this. The programs become codified and the meaning or rationale behind them non-existent (or at least forgotten). One simply does it because it's "supposed to be that way." This is important to note, because our programs become prioritized in church life, and our practice then tells people that they are to conform to the program, rather than the other way around. New churches typically start without any programs, and thus, as a result, prioritize the people they encounter. Programming comes later when the need presents itself in community life, and the purpose is understood.

> Growing churches value people over programs.

This really can't be overstated. Growing churches value people over programs. Every visitor who visits your church can tell what is more important…can you? Yes, every church values both people and programs to some degree…but which do you value more? Only a mega-church is able to "pull off" the focus on programs without losing enough relational impact to hurt it. (People attending mega-churches are looking for something different than people who attend smaller, but still growing, churches.) Most churches have to acknowledge that people, especially visitors, guests and new members, are not as valued as their own programming and ministries.

By the way, the programming in your church will determine, to some degree, the people you attract to your church. How well you are able to provide the programming in question will influence their decision to return or not. However, the relationships they make—or don't make—will be the real determining factor in whether they stay or go. Programming MAY get them there, but unless you are a mega-church, it won't be what keeps them there.

INFORMAL GATHERINGS

New churches rely more on unplanned, spontaneous networking and get-togethers than planned events. These promote relational activity, but typically they are developed individual-to-individual or family-to-family. These relational activities are often initiated through worship or small group/Sunday School experiences, but are cultivated out of the desire to build upon these new relationships and enable them to go deeper. Because there are not as many programming opportunities for people to get together, individuals and families make more plans on their own and find personalized ways to be mutually beneficial for each other.

This last point is especially powerful, as each one involved is able to imprint the relationship in a customized, personal way. For example, an individual may decide to develop a relationship at a coffee shop, on the golf course or at a garden party. Families may choose to go to the beach together, visit an amusement park or invite each other over for dinner. The variations are limitless and the solutions are handpicked. A lack of programming from the church, while still emphasizing relationships, largely makes this happen.

So how does a new church maximize the relationship quotient? Often it is a subconscious process, built upon the reality that there are smaller numbers of people in the congregation as a whole. This enables everyone to have the opportunity to get to know each other, because they are easily aware of all others in the group. Awareness to others and a smaller number of potential total relationships enable everyone who "sticks" to feel better known (subjective, to be sure, but this is felt primarily at the emotive level) than if they were surrounded by hundreds of unknown people in a mega-church. The complexity of relationship possibilities are taken away, and with it comes the psychological freedom (or necessity?) to go deeper in relationship with those who are in the new church.

You would think that this would be true of small, older churches, too. After all, they don't have complex relationship equations, either. Unfortunately, though, there is not the same dynamic at work relationally in this situation. Here's why. Older churches have two factors working against them in regard to relationships: their current system and the familiarity of those already there. The current system includes predictable programming, with weekly and annual events that members anticipate for relationship-building opportunities, as well as facility-based experiences, which become the setting for most relationship development. In addition, the familiarity of long-standing friendships, the roles these individuals hold in church life and even where they can be found when they are in the church building (classroom, pew, etc.) mitigate against the informality of new relationships forming. Routine relational patterns have taken root and individuals are not eager to change them.

There is a conscious relationship-building process in some new churches, too. Church plants understand the importance that relationships have in bringing, and keeping, new people in a church. Researchers suggest that visitors decide whether they will return to a congregation in the first seven minutes of their initial visit. However, if they attend at least twice, then the chances are high that they will stay connected to your church…for at least four to six months.[36] What will keep newcomers with the church longer are the relationships they develop. If they are able to develop seven significant relationships in those first six months, the chances are great that they will remain indefinitely. If they don't, well, let's just say, they won't be around for someone to find out why they departed.[37]

> What will keep newcomers with the church longer are the relationships they develop.

Some new churches go so far as to implement a "two minute rule," suggesting that for the first two minutes after the worship experience ends each week, regular attendees spend time seeking out and planting the seeds of relationship with those they do not yet know well. This informal chaos encourages new friendships to be developed spontaneously; it simply provides the "quick connect" environment that facilitates such relationship-building to begin.

As SonRise Church on the eastern shore of Maryland began, they budgeted for their staff to take guests out for a meal or coffee after the weekly Sunday worship time had ended. These leaders were encouraged to seek out visitors and when they were discovered, the staff invited them to join their family for food and fellowship. Many accepted the offer and began forming initial relationships that brought them back again to become a part of the new church. Informal gatherings, like this, take place because leaders have been intentional about making the most of relationships.

LIMITED STRUCTURE

The bigger a church gets, the more likely it will function like a business and not a family. The reason for this is simple: size and age foster complexity in living organisms. As more people join a church, simple, informal processes are felt inadequate to handle the number of people now involved. Structures, with formal processes and procedures, are implemented to organize the congregation more effectively. The larger and/or older the church, the more complicated the structure and procedures become. This is because human beings have a tendency to always "add" more to what already exists, rather than "subtract" from what is already there. More is thought to be better.

These particular assumptions—that more is better and that a church will function more effectively like a business than as a family—rival the value and importance new churches place on relationships. Structure is shunned whenever possible, keeping the congregation functioning simply and easily. Business decisions (every church must deal with some of these) are minimized and dealt with more like a family would deal with its own household decisions, rather than as a business managed by a CEO or a company with stockholders.

> Structure functions best, when like the human skeleton, it does its job effectively but remains unseen.

Structure, in and of itself, is neither good nor bad. Its purpose is to produce efficiency and to anticipate objectively what needs to be done for the benefit of the church. It functions best, when like the human skeleton, it does its job effectively but remains unseen. However, it all too often provides hurdles or barriers that are unknown to most of the people in the church until they step on the tripwires affected. The structure fails to be permission-giving, and instead is a permission-withholding process.

Businesses often minimize the characteristics that make family the powerful social unit it is in society. Emotions—including love—are neglected; unity is desired, but unnecessary; and, productivity is all that matters. To that end, relationships don't make a difference; in fact, they can get in the way. They can sway decisions and can be counter-productive to the desired outcome, which is progress and growth.

The only problem with this thinking is that the fastest-growing congregations don't make these assumptions. In fact, they would argue against them. New churches—which grow faster than all other age-churches—have limited structure and fail to function like a business! The rule of thumb is this: don't structure beyond the current need. Anything else is unwanted and eventually unhelpful. And as for family: the more you can enhance the positive familial relationships in church life, the deeper, richer and healthier a church community will be.

Later in this book there will be more about the role of structure in church life. Suffice it to say for now: don't let assumptions impact your relationships or growth. Validate them through experience.

WORD-OF-MOUTH MARKETING

There are a lot of people in church life today who don't like the word "marketing." It sounds too commercial, too consumer, too secular. Granted, the concept carries baggage in our capitalistic Western world today. Regardless, whatever you call it, the reality still exists: impressions and perceptions will affect how others see your local church. What each church planter must determine is who will deliver to his "audience" the impressions and perceptions they will form about the new church, and how they will receive this information.

Marketing techniques change with the times. From Yellow Pages and newspaper advertisements in the 1960s to social media and Internet websites today, new churches have attempted to inform others about their presence in the community. But while methods have altered dramatically through the years due to new technologies, word-of-mouth "marketing" has stood the test of time, no matter where, by whom or when the message has been presented. The reason this is so, I believe, can be found in the fact it is based on relational connections. The credibility of the messenger is tied to the message, and the message is delivered to those persons one knows.

Consistently, researchers say that the number one reason people visit or participate in a church is because someone they know and respect invited them. The statistics suggest some eighty percent of new attendees engage a church for this very reason. Elmer Towns and the *Church Growth Institute* have made much of this reality over the years. Their *"FRIEND DAY"* campaign materials are built off of the premise that if everyone simply encouraged one friend or neighbor to attend worship with them one week, attendance would double. Many of these guests, so the assumption continues, will return in coming weeks.[38]

    This is the power of relationships.
    It validates the message.
    It underscores the message.
    It interests the recipient.
    It attracts the recipient.
    It produces impact and results.

New churches, with limited resources, make the most of word-of-mouth marketing techniques. They suggest that members look first to those in their circles of relational influence to tell about Christ and the new church of which they are a part. These circles would include family, friends, co-workers, neighbors, and the like. Because they already have a relationship with them, these individuals and families are more likely to respond affirmatively to an invitation or participation in something the church has to offer. And when they eventually show up, they won't be strangers, because their friend is already there.

In new churches, this enhances evangelism efforts, too, since many new believers only have unbelieving friends with whom to share. As a result, new churches that maximize relationships and encourage word-of-mouth opportunities see more people commit to following Christ, and subsequently see more growth in the church plant during the early years. If leaders disciple these new believers intentionally in the early years, the trend will continue; if not, they will follow the tendency of most believers to stop hanging out with their lost friends, and the opportunities will stop…and so will the growth.

NEXT STEPS

APPLY TO YOUR SETTING

Examine the relationship-webs of your church, illustrating who is connected to whom. Build a diagram, much like a genealogical tree. Note the key individuals who are responsible for connecting many of the people to the new church. Determine how they made that happen and maximize the lessons learned.

Evaluate the programming in your new church, along with the anticipated, desired programming also being considered. Consider the reason why they exist (the objective they should accomplish); align them with the church's purpose and vision; otherwise, terminate them.

Determine if your structure is efficient, by evaluating whether or not the processes, procedures and organizational "how to" steps draw attention to themselves or move people effectively to the results needed.

Figure out more ways to maximize relationship-building through your new church. Explore or bless activities that are interactive, rather than passive, in nature. Budget time and money to support these efforts.

GOOD QUESTIONS TO ASK

1. In what ways do we demonstrate that we value people over programs? How could we improve this perception, as well as the reality?

2. How do we maximize the power of relationships in our new church? When are people able to go deeper with others? How are new people able to make connections with those who are already here?

3. How effectively and efficiently are we handling the decision-making process of the church? What could we do to improve the relational impact of our structure?

4. How are we using "word-of-mouth" marketing to our advantage in this new church?

5. How are we keeping our people connected to their lost and unchurched friends around them?

DIGGING DEEPER

Cole, Neil. *Organic Church*. San Francisco, CA: Jossey-Bass Publishers, 2005.

Holladay, Tom. *The Relationship Principles of Jesus*. Grand Rapids, MI: Zondervan, 2008.

Maxwell, John. *Winning with People*. Nashville, TN: Thomas Nelson, 2004.

McIntosh, Gary L. *Beyond the First Visit*. Grand Rapids, MI: Baker Books, 2006.

Millwood, Randy. *To Love and To Cherish From This Day Forward*. Owings Mills, MD: simplymillwood, 2010.

Towns, Elmer. *FRIEND DAY Resource Packet with CDs*. Elkton, MD: Ephesians 4 Ministries/Church Growth Institute, 2011a.

7

Kingdom Citizens

Pastor Joe had arrived in a town where there were already many churches ("What town in America doesn't already have churches?" Joe thought to himself). A handful of these churches were clearly recognized as an evangelical presence in the community, and as he came to find out, a couple of them were making a significant impact for Christ.

In the early weeks after his arrival in the town, Pastor Joe set appointments and visited with each of the pastors in the community. His goal was threefold: to get to know them as colleagues in ministry, to glean wisdom from their years of experience in town and to let each of them know that he and Redemption Fellowship were not here to "steal" their members, but to join their churches in reaching the yet unreached in the community for Jesus.

Joe felt this last point was an important message to share with each of them. He was not interested in "reaching the already reached," as he explained in his conversations with them ("Rearranging the chairs on the deck of the Titanic," was the way one of the pastors had ominously put it). "There are plenty of lost people to go around," Joe believed, with no need or desire to focus on those believers already active in another church.

To be honest, Pastor Joe's appointments were met with two very different reactions. On the one hand, there were a few pastors who were critical of Joe's presence, stating the town "already had enough churches" and "a newcomer won't make a difference here." Their defensive and adversarial response to Joe had been unwanted, but not totally unexpected. He had been warned in seminary that some pastors would see him as "competition." On the other hand, the church planter found a few allies among the fraternity of community pastors, who were excited by his presence and welcomed him to the community with open arms. They invariably had a Kingdom mindset and an evangelistic heart.

Pastor Joe was convinced that the synergy of their joint ministries in the community, and whatever cooperative Kingdom impact they could make, would magnify Jesus and multiply the difference the Church (with a capital C) would make in the town...and maybe, even around the world. "My denominational label is a part of my roots, my heritage," Joe would tell them, "and I am thankful for that. But the Gospel transcends my heritage, and yours, too. If we Christ-followers are ever going to fulfill the mission our Lord commanded, we must find ways to make it our most significant endeavor of all."

Church planters are Kingdom citizens. They live and serve far beyond their own needs and that of their singular congregation. They seek to enlarge and extend the Kingdom, whatever it takes. Typically, this priority will take their actions beyond the boundaries of their own walls and likely, beyond the boundaries of their own denominational "tribe," as well.

This characteristic of effective new churches appears, at first glance, to be counter-intuitive; it doesn't make logical sense. Why would planters want to focus on more than just their own church? Aren't there enough needs and concerns in that congregation to occupy a church planting leader's full attention?

The answer, of course, is obvious; certainly there are enough needs within any given church planting effort to take all of one's energy, and then some. However, this reality doesn't convey the whole story. Planters see the value in helping fellow pastors and planters, and in learning from them, too.

They recognize that they are not in competition with those also pastoring and planting. Other Bible-believing, Gospel-preaching leaders, and the churches they serve, are on the same team. They are striving to reach the lost and unchurched with the Good News of Jesus Christ, too. Their success fuels the success of all. Thus, collaboration, not competition, is the order of the day.

LOYALTY AND BRAND NAMES

Some people become anxious when they realize that church planters, and younger ministers in general, demonstrate no "brand" loyalty to the denomination of which they are a part. They worry that planters who lack loyalty to their organization will erode its support, and eventually its influence. These same people believe that such attitudes jeopardize the survival of their denomination or organization. Attempts to sustain their own survival at any cost, though, belie institutionalism and bureaucracy. It is small-sighted and selfish.

It is true that denominations are struggling today, in part, because of this shift among younger generations and church planters away from "blind" brand name loyalty. However, if one digs deeper, he or she will find that what new, young leaders and planters are looking for is "what's behind the mirror." They want to see and understand the values that make an organization "tick," including behaviors that reinforce those values and not contradict them or simply work for self-preservation.

> Church planters are not "anti-denominational..." However, they remember what others may easily forget: the denomination exists for the local church, not *visa versa*.

Church planters are not "anti-denominational," in my opinion. In point of fact, more of them are connected to a denomination than not. However, they remember what others may easily forget: the denomination exists for the local church, not *visa versa*. Planters are rarely interested in the politics, the business (other than the God-given mission) and the programs of their tribe. Moreover, if it is not biblical, functional and "on mission," then they often believe it has outlived its usefulness and provides little or no value—only headaches and hurdles—to them and the churches they are starting.

On the other hand, planters long for relationships, networks and collegiality to support them in their ministry endeavor. They seek denominations and organizations that will embrace them for who they are and that will help them achieve their potential in church planting. However, if they don't find this kind of denomination or organization, most of them will create networks or alliances—formally or informally—to provide many of the same benefits without the encumbrance of bureaucracy and institutionalism.

Church planters are not interested in promoting or perpetuating a denomination or a "brand" of Christianity; rather, they are passionate about Jesus and joining Him in extending the Kingdom of God.

If a denomination or network values this, planters will want to be a part; if not, its future will be devoid of young, entrepreneurial church starters who believe that the Kingdom of God is the only genuine way to bring transformation to our world today.

BIG-PICTURE PERSPECTIVE

All of this is to say that church planters, especially in their earlier days, have a much larger perspective on God's work than simply the ministry of their own church plants. Perhaps it would be more accurate to say, they tend to have a "broader" perspective, for their vision is wide, seeing locally and globally what God is doing and finding ways to partner with Him in that work. This type of vision is "bifocal," seeing beyond the limitations that many long-time church leaders see.

They see beyond their geography.
They see beyond their ethnicity.
They see beyond their socio-economic status.
They see beyond their "tribal distinctions."
They see far beyond their own local churches.
They long to see as God sees.

Part of this reality is due to the fact that they don't actually have church families of their own...yet. As a result, they see through more idealized lens as they perceive the world around them. This becomes more difficult as they partner with God in seeing the new church come to fruition. As membership grows and the needs of new parishioners cry out for attention, the local congregation becomes more dominant in the mind and heart of the planter, as well as all of the church.

The wise planter refuses to let this distract him or the congregation from staying focused on the big-picture, Kingdom perspective of what God is doing and how their collective life together plugs into this ultimate reality. The planter challenges the family of faith to think bigger, see further, feel wider than simply the church they are planting together. He redirects them to the Kingdom beyond and to the world around them, as yet unreached. He reminds them of those who have paved the way for their lives years before, as well as the legacy they will leave for others to follow.

> **This surfaces an important truth: new churches want to make a difference and believe they can, even from their earliest days.**

In our last church plant, our church family started funding other church plants right away, within our first year's budget. We helped five such church plants over the six years I was their planter/pastor. In addition to local mission efforts for our own congregation and for these church plants in the metropolitan area, we sent a mission team to Europe. And with our own departure, Community Church had sent out five appointed and commissioned missionaries, three overseas and two in the States.

This kind of big-picture perspective guides the planter and new church in all areas of decision-making and lifestyle. They typically set up their initial budgets to reflect funding for missions and church planting endeavors. They establish direct missions efforts, often overseas, within their first year. They find local ministry impact sites and organizations, and they link arms with them through volunteer efforts and even financial contributions. They are eager to help the less fortunate in their communities as advocates for social justice issues.

While some or even all of this may not be unique to this era, what is unusual is that the determination of the organizations and individuals they help are rarely discovered or implemented purely along denominational, tribal lines. Rather, they help those within the larger Kingdom where they feel their new church can make the greatest impact and where they find evidence that the organizations or individuals involved "have their act together." That is to say, these organizations are credible and knowledgeable in what they are doing. They have demonstrated these realities sufficiently enough to satisfy the new church's curiosity. This surfaces an important truth: new churches want to make a difference and believe they can, even from their earliest days. In some ways, their involvement in "big-picture" Kingdom concerns validates their own existence and can gain further community and evangelical supporters, beyond their own tribe.

In fact, tribal leaders, at both the local church and denominational levels, may question their legitimacy—and certainly, their loyalty—more than outsiders, since they rarely promote "the company line." And while the new church and its planter will garner its own critics from within the denomination or tradition of which they are a part, the wise leader knows this is to be expected of (1) anyone who bucks the conventional way things have been done, and (2) attempts anything innovative and "outside the box," a characteristic already noted to be typical of church planters.

Big-picture thinkers lead their new churches to be big-picture subjects. They refuse to live in a parochial, narrow-minded world, constrained by the belief that a world of ministry within the church equates to the totality of Kingdom living needed or desired. The broad perspective enables the new church to spread its roots deeper for strength and its branches wider for impact. It goes so far as to believe the fruit of its efforts will be carried by the wind to other places and peoples where they will experience the impact of Kingdom citizens, living out their calling as fully as possible.

COOPERATIVE AROUND THE LARGER MISSION

Every <u>new</u> church understands its own purpose for existence. Unfortunately, not every church does, at least not anymore. At one point, at least in the earliest days, each church knew why it was born and set about doing what God had planted it to do. And as we've already seen, church plants have big dreams, because they believe in a big God. They are convinced that God has much He wants to do through them that will make a difference in lives, families and communities—even around the world.

As a result, they realize early in their genesis that the "mission" is larger than what they alone can accomplish. They will seek out kindred spirits and partner with them in ways that they could not do on their own.

They will work together on a mission trip overseas.

They will share in giving to a worthy, needy cause.

They will hold joint evangelistic efforts or activities in their communities.

They will build a broad base of people who will intercede together.

They will join in shared worship experiences.

The Southern Baptist Convention has championed a "kindred spirit" for almost ninety years through a shared giving process, known as the Cooperative Program. Begun in 1925, individual churches cooperatively share a portion of their tithes and offerings, so that collectively these churches can make greater Kingdom impact than they could ever do individually. The money is distributed to mission work, both domestic and international, as well as to its seminaries (and a small bit elsewhere). As a result, the Southern Baptist Convention today boasts the largest Protestant missions force in the world, along with the largest number of seminary students. This is a direct result of the collective ministry of so many churches working together.[39]

However, the interesting thing, at least in my experience, is that today kindred spirits and partners are not always tribally defined. Rather than being ones from the same denomination or faith tradition, they are often made up of ones who are sharing similar experiences in life (i.e., other church planters) or going through the same seasons in life (e.g., age or familial experience). The same commonality that draws individuals to new churches in turn draws their leaders to cooperate together around the greater mission of Jesus Christ.

As a result, planters are redefining the filters of cooperation. This is not unlike previous generations, except in the actual filters used. No longer are the filters such characteristics as "denomination," "geography" or "methodology;" rather, they are commonality of experience and Kingdom values, including "passion for the lost," "innovations in effective ministry" and often, "social justice."

> "Every generation must own what they will do and how they will do it for themselves."

One of my mentors, Bob Brindle, told me years ago, "Every generation must own what they will do and how they will do it for themselves." Bob was right. Planters will own cooperation as a value, but on their own terms.

CREATIVE ALLIANCES

This enables creative alliances and networks among planters, in which they learn from each other and sharpen each other. These alliances strengthen their efforts and shape their initiatives. They create collegial cohorts, rather than competitive rivals, in ministry.

Most planters seek out these alliances. Church planters and their young congregations dominate national groups, such as the *Willow Creek Association*, *Acts 29* and the broader *Exponential* community. Other newer groups, like *Ecclesia* and the *Sojourn Network*, do much the same. On a regional, local scale, planters will seek out or form such networks for the same kind of collegial support. These may come into existence for a variety of reasons, but what typically glues them together is a peer effort, initiative or experience to which each participant can relate. It may be as broad as the entire church planting experience or as narrow as a collaborative church planting effort in their own community, but something "connects" them to each other. This transcends their "differences" in denomination, methodology and often, even theology.

Daryl McCready saw a need in the small town of Berlin, Maryland, which his church could not directly address: a burgeoning Hispanic population. McCready knew that the key to reaching the Hispanics in his area successfully relied on finding the right Hispanic church planter to come and establish a church to reach the growing number of residents who only spoke Spanish. Daryl challenged his association of churches and his local ministerial alliance to develop this project together. Two other churches—both from other denominational traditions—chose to participate and contributed to assist in this effort. Nuevo Amanecer with Pastor Alexis Vides has been established in Berlin as a result of this creative alliance. Since then, McCready's church has gone on to support fifteen other church plants, including six outside their denominational tradition.

This type of networking enables planters to stay focused on the harvest field, keeps them sharp and draws on their unconventional nature. It helps them be more effective in reaching the lost for Jesus. And it provides them with more

> **Citizenship within that Kingdom is shared equally. It is lived interdependently.**

"tangible" evidence that they are "pushing back the darkness" and joining Jesus in ushering in transformation within their community. This effectiveness, in and of itself, then motivates them to further alliances and network efforts in making a difference for the Kingdom.

This networking is seen in peer learning communities, too. In Montgomery County, Maryland, many evangelical church planters for some time have been gathering together monthly. They do this for many reasons, including prayer and emotional support, advice and counsel, learning and friendship. They function in the same way as *"iron sharpens iron"* (Proverbs 27:17), to challenge and improve each other, and as a result, to strengthen the Kingdom of God.

Learning communities, training opportunities and missions endeavors all happen within the bounds of one's own denomination or tradition, too. Many times, in fact, they happen very effectively. It is not the "trans-denominational" element that makes them productive; rather, it is the spirit shared by those who participate. They recognize they are on "the front lines" in ministry. They need allies in the battle. No one church can go it alone.

Thus, cooperation replaces competition. They live life together as a band of brothers. "Thy Kingdom" trumps "my kingdom." Citizenship within that Kingdom is shared equally. It is lived interdependently.

And that's what makes the difference.

NEXT STEPS

APPLY TO YOUR SETTING

Look "behind the mirror" of the denomination, tribe or network of which your new church is a part. Examine their values. See if their behaviors are aligned with yours at a values level, not just at a theological level.

Evaluate your new church for Kingdom elements that go beyond or transcend the scope of your single congregation. Reject selfishness and territorialism. Look for ways to assist in Kingdom growth within your community and elsewhere.

Consider ways to network with other church planters, within or beyond your tribe. Commit to assist each other in keeping a Kingdom perspective and staying focused on the mission of God.

Note where God is at work around you.[40] Join Him in that work, without reservation.

GOOD QUESTIONS TO ASK

1. *Why are you connected to the groups with whom you are networked? Why do they do what they do?*

2. *In what ways do you cooperate with others within your denomination? Beyond your denomination? What determines what you do and with whom you do it?*

3. *What steps do you need to take to have "Kingdom vision?" What might your church do differently as a result?*

4. *What are the "non-negotiables" that would keep you from being able to work together cooperatively with others in Kingdom work?*

5. Where are you finding "iron sharpens iron" in your own life? Who supports and assists you in the midst of your church planting journey?

6. What Kingdom efforts will you lead your new church to do over the next twelve months?

DIGGING DEEPER

Ferguson, Dave & Ferguson, Jon. *Exponential.* Grand Rapids, MI: Zondervan, 2010.

Friesen, Dwight J. *Thy Kingdom Connected.* Grand Rapids, MI: Baker Books, 2004.

Godin, Seth. *Tribes.* New York, NY: Portfolio, 2008.

Stetzer, Ed. *Subversive Kingdom.* Nashville, TN: B & H Publishing Group, 2012.

Budget and Time Priorities

"Can I have your attention, please? All of you?" Pastor Joe asked. It was the quarterly meeting of his leadership team at the church, and he had suddenly lost control of the group. The pastor had been overviewing the calendar of events for the coming quarter, and Tom, a new member of Redemption Fellowship, had asked why they weren't scheduling more events and activities for the members of the church. The implication, it seemed, was that the church was too focused on the unreached people of the community and not focused enough on the needs of the congregation.

At this point the group had all started talking to each other, and nobody could understand anyone. Once Pastor Joe had recaptured everyone's attention, he responded. "Tom, that's a great question; let me try to answer it. When Redemption Fellowship began, the focus was completely on the unreached people of our community. That burden and the accompanying vision is what brought this church into being. In fact, that sharp focus is what has enabled us to be successful and grow so quickly over this first year. If—or when—we lose that focus and shift our priorities elsewhere, our growth will slow or stop, and our 'reason for being' will have changed. As a result, we must continue to keep our time—and money—prioritized to reach the unreached."

Tom mumbled something inaudible as he feigned protest (he was, after all, coming from another church in the community where the calendar and budget focused on the people already in the congregation). In the pause, Harold spoke up, "But don't we have a responsibility to disciple these new people, not just reach them?" Pastor Joe smiled; "Harold gets it," he thought.

"Why, absolutely!" the pastor replied. "That's totally the point, isn't it? To disciple them, we must reach them and allow the Holy Spirit the room to do His regenerative work on their lives first. When He does, we must find ways to facilitate His growth within their lives. That should happen through the ongoing strategies of the church process: small groups, one-on-one discipling relationships and of course, our worship experiences…but also through getting them involved right away in reaching out to the unreached, too. It's kind of an 'on the job training' opportunity.

"It would be a mistake to spend so much time simply on 'us;' we can't be the church God intended if we're not missional. And we can't be missional, if we're not seeing beyond ourselves. In fact, I'm convinced that we can't be fully devoted disciples unless we're in the harvest fields where Jesus wants us to be.

"And that brings me to our budgeting of money, too. One of the telltale signs of a plateaued or declining church is how little money they spend on outreach. Most churches have less than five percent of their income budgeted for outreach…not to be confused with missions, which they typically understand to be beyond their own community. In fact, these same churches are so loaded down with fixed expenses that they have little flexibility to maneuver fiscally; they often don't even have twenty percent of their budget for ministry of any kind! On the other hand, here at our new church, Redemption Fellowship, we spent over fifty percent of our budget in year one for outreach. We are preparing for year two, and it still looks like we'll be able to put somewhere near thirty to thirty-five percent toward outreach. Let me ask all of you: do you think these priorities are making a difference for us in reaching so many new people?" The group all nodded their affirmation. "Then that's why we can't afford to change these priorities, just to make us more comfortable or feel better about ourselves."

Time and money: there aren't two more important words to most people in our world today than these. For churches, this is often true, too. In fact, more churches split over these things, or the subsequent manifestations of these priorities, than anything else. How we spend our time and our money says so much about what we truly value in life. While churches often purport to hold biblical values of evangelism, prayer and ministry, their checkbook and calendar—like our own—suggest otherwise.

This is a significant point. Where you invest your time and money reflects your heart. Your own priorities and values are visible for others to see. Young churches place such a high premium on reaching others with the Gospel and assimilating them into a disciple-making church lifestyle that they have little time for anything else. And this is part of what makes them grow so quickly and so well.

AROUND MISSION

Budget and calendar concerns start with a focus on mission. Church leaders understand why they exist and resource accordingly. They make sure that the activities they place on the calendar all contribute to the accomplishment of this mission. Leaders freely challenge any event they are unsure will assist them in the achievement of God's purpose for the new church. This analysis keeps them centered on the mission they have been given and their stewardship responsibility in fulfilling it.

They are meticulous in evaluation, reviewing activities they have recently completed in an attempt to make sure these have accomplished the purpose for which they were intended. If these activities have moved them closer to the

> Mission, vision and values become the primary filters for a church plant in determining what it should be doing and then, how to fund it.

success of the mission, they may be repeated. If it has unexpectedly distracted or distanced them from the mission, effective church planters will not repeat it. Nothing the church does is beyond scrutiny. In this way, the fledgling congregation is able to stay transfixed upon the mission and vision God has given it.

Resources follow strategy. In other words, once plans are made that will help the new church to move closer to the ultimate success of the mission, then and only then are dollars made available to support it. The use of money by the congregation as a whole is seen as a stewardship, in which God has entrusted them to make wise decisions that will further His mission in the world. Community is built around the mission, not apart from it. Disciples are made in the work of the mission, not separated from it.

Mission, vision and values become the primary filters for a church plant in determining what it should be doing and then, how to fund it. Personalities can't determine this (even the pastor/planter!); nor should tradition (what's been done in the past) decide it. In a new church, limited resources make such filters a necessity; otherwise, resourcing will be wasted and opportunities missed.

EVANGELISM AND OUTREACH

Focused strategy around the mission will invariably lead a church outside its proverbial walls to the unreached people of the community. I say proverbial walls, because most church plants don't have actual walls of their own. In my opinion, this makes it easier to see the unreached people all around them and to make plans with them in mind. Prioritizing the unreached in planning require the focus to remain beyond these walls.

When this is the mental attitude and passion of the people, the thrust of the church's ministry is always on evangelism and outreach. Its heart beats with the lost around it; its vision is always scanning the horizon; its hands and feet are always ready to move, for the sake of others. It bleeds redemption, reconciliation and restoration. It agonizes and strategizes over ways to get the Gospel to more people around them, so that they can know the love and power of a relationship with Jesus Christ, too.

So a church plant plans accordingly. In its months of incubation (before it actually "launches," a term used typically to define the start of regular worship experiences), almost all of its activity is focused outward. (The only exception would be core or launch team development.) After the launch of worship, the new church tends to scale back some on its outwardly-focused scheduling. The addition of small groups and the worship experience itself add regular, scheduled opportunities that should attempt to integrate newcomers seamlessly into the new church, too. However, these calendar-intensive activities typically are focused internally on those who are already in the church.

In such cases, most new churches attempt to calendar virtually everything else toward outreach and evangelism efforts. Time commitments (they are already asking members and regular attendees to give up two to four hours a week for worship and small group involvement) and funding limitations (the budget now has to support the above activities, too) curtail the evangelism efforts. However, with intentionality and passion, outreach can still be a major objective for the new congregation. Budgets and calendars usually result in somewhere between 25-35 percent of all the new church does still being focused on outreach and evangelism.

> **Budgets and calendars usually result in somewhere between 25-35 percent of all the new church does still being focused on outreach and evangelism.**

This is very different from most established churches. Programming by ages and specialized affinity groups dilutes the outreach efforts of the church in two ways. It leaves less money in the budget for such ministries, and it adds to an ever-increasing schedule of commitments for members to their church, leaving less discretionary time available for those who might have helped otherwise.

So how do new churches "do" evangelism and outreach? Certainly, they don't do it in the typical, traditional ways most of us imagine when we consider "evangelism." Rarely is it confrontational, at all. Instead, the strategies typically include some or all of the following: regular servant evangelism activities, block parties for the neighborhood or community, seminars, retreats, other outings, and relational, friendship evangelism initiatives in homes, neighborhoods or at the workplace. Often small groups or worship experiences have an evangelistic component to them, as well.

Servant evangelism activities (also known as "acts of kindness" or something similar) are a preferred on-going way to share Christ with one's community. There are literally scores of such activities that can be performed to help others with a small touch of kindness. These acts, which range from free car washes to paying down gasoline purchases to mowing lawns, are all efforts, as Steve Sjogren likes to put it, "to show the love of Christ in a practical, relevant way."[41] Verbal testimonies are not offered and Gospel presentations are not given unless, and only if, individuals ask and continue to be interested in knowing what prompts the church to act in such a way as this. (Of course, if asked, then participants from the new church are eager and ready to share the Good News.) Rather, these events are often simply "seed planting" experiences in evangelism; they build credibility, authenticity and relevance for the new church; they foster a burden for the lost, respect for every person and a dependence upon God for believers who are involved.

Block parties are often an introductory way for a new church to announce its presence in a community, or to be a "good neighbor" to residents they have yet to meet. Infinity Church in Laurel, Maryland, has used these events extensively over the years to reach new people and to plant seeds of the Gospel in the lives of community residents, as opportunity presents itself. These events are usually multiple hours on a weekend day and involve lots of on-going activity for all age groups, especially children. Such block parties have musicians, artists and other performers share during the day. There is always lots of food to be enjoyed by all.

Testimonies are sometimes shared and Bibles given away at block party experiences. Audience participants are told they can learn more about Jesus, the church or the Bible, at an information table or if they will simply ask one of the block party hosts. Because block parties are a "come and go" event, they serve more as an evangelism awareness tool that can lead to credibility in the community and further opportunities for evangelism in follow-up.

Seminars, retreats and outings are occasionally used by new churches in an intentional—though rarely, overt—evangelistic way. Training on parenting, dealing with finances or scrapbooking events are held with story opportunities and Christian witness being shared. Retreats, where unreached individuals are invited to participate, may share evangelistic testimonies or videos. Occasionally, they may be even more explicitly evangelistic, for example, in churches using the *Alpha* course as a part of their strategy. Other outings, like trips to see an evangelistic movie, hear a believing celebrity when he or she visits the city, or even to join the new church on a mission trip endeavor, all provide varying levels of evangelistic opportunity.

Added to these community efforts are the relational, one-on-one experiences of individuals and families in their daily lives. Conversations over the fence between neighbors or at the water cooler in the office can lead to longer evangelistic opportunities over lunch or a home-cooked meal. Invitations and sharing can lead these contacts to participate in a small group setting or a worship experience, too, where they can hear the Gospel or encounter the claims of Christ in a way that would evoke a response.

MISSIONS INVOLVEMENT

New churches also budget for missions involvement from the very beginning, almost without exception. This is more than the typical "praying and giving" efforts of many churches. Church plants are started with the belief that they must be intentional about being involved in missions, not just by proxy, but also in person.

This emphasis actually predates the recent emphasis on being a "missional church," though church plants have readily adopted this terminology. For decades now, church plants have practiced what they teach: our God is a missionary God, and He calls us to be a missionary people who join Him on His mission. Thus, they plan missions experiences—locally and internationally—early in the life of the new church. They may help a soup kitchen or Habitat for Humanity in their own community. They will often take a team on an overseas trip to help the underprivileged in an impoverished, third-world country by building a school or digging a well.

Church plants, always eager for participants, often welcome non-members and sometimes, even pre-Christians on such missions efforts. Surprised? Many unbelieving people in our society today want to be personally involved in humanitarian efforts, and they see the church's missions efforts from this perspective (if they know about it, at all). New churches capitalize on this by gaining participation and the opportunity to live and share the Gospel with others as a part of such an effort. Leaders are confident that their team's devotion to God, their passion to help people in need and the authenticity of their own lives will lead these unbelieving participants, as well as those whom they have come to serve, into a faith relationship with Christ.

> Missions experiences always energize and embolden those who participate in them evangelistically.

Missions experiences always energize and embolden those who participate in them evangelistically. When we took the first mission team from our church plant on the South Shore of Boston to Europe, our team trained with energy and passion for the evangelistic opportunities that might come our way. On the field, we were motivated by our mission and the clock (We might never see this person again!), and as a result, shared the Gospel freely. We had a level of courage, as well as opportunity, of which we were unaware in the States. And it made a difference in the lives of many.

This can translate back to the "home field" of one's own communities, if the new church capitalizes upon it. Local ministry opportunities that are comparable to what was experienced as a part of their mission field experience, whenever possible, will build upon the trip, with the potential for long-lasting impact. New churches often later determine to make these the focal point of their "niche" in evangelistic outreach locally.

In addition, most new churches also budget for future church planting involvement as a "parent" or "partner" church. While giving to other denominational or parachurch/missions organizations, they often additionally set aside one or two percent of their income for these church planting endeavors. They believe the Scripture teaches that all living things God has created are intended to reproduce, and that includes the Church, a living organism, for it is the Body of Christ. As with personal missions involvement, they desire to have hands-on experience in this, as an outworking of their biblical understanding of God's mission and our missional responsibility before Him to the world.

While most new churches don't help start another church as early as originally desired, a large majority eventually do get personally involved in seeing a new congregation come into being. And if church planting truly is "the most effective evangelistic methodology under heaven," then this too, is a part of their outreach strategy, even though it may not benefit them numerically or financially. Jesus taught His followers, *"Whoever wants to save his life will lose it"* (Mark 8:35). New churches willingly sacrifice, because of their great faith in God and the recognition that others sacrificed for them, too, or they wouldn't even exist at all.

FIXED EXPENSES

One reason new churches are able to budget larger amounts of time and money for outreach and evangelism is because they have fewer fixed expenses than the long-established church. Most of a typical church's budget goes toward facility (debt retirement, insurance and maintenance) and personnel (staff compensation plus benefits). These items, while certainly vital, crowd out a larger portion of resources for use in ministry, and especially in outreach. These items can easily occupy seventy-five to eighty percent of a church's budget. Add to these amounts the missions funding in the budget of the church and there can be little left for use in ministry.

In terms of time, established churches ask members to participate in one to three worship experiences a week, plus a typical small group or Sunday School gathering. When you factor in other age-graded or affinity groups (e.g., senior adults, youth, choir, etc.) and administrative/leadership involvement (especially on committees and boards), many churches leave little time for their members to do anything else in ministry.

New churches have an advantage here, when viewed from the perspective of fixed time and money expenses. Few have mortgages or have to worry about utility bills and maintenance costs. Even fewer have a programming schedule that requires individuals to participate regularly in more than one worship experience, a small group and possibly one leadership or affinity group meeting weekly.

> The principle here should be obvious: wait as long as you can before committing the new church to additional, on-going fixed expenses, especially when it comes to facilities.

Such a streamlined budget and schedule leave much more opportunity for outreach and evangelism, a fact obvious to all who understand the reasons new churches grow so effectively.

The principle here should be obvious: wait as long as you can before committing the new church to additional, on-going fixed expenses, especially when it comes to facilities. It will slow down growth and evangelistic outreach. Rick Warren likes to say, "The shoe must never tell the foot how big it can grow."[42] Even adding additional staff, if not done correctly, will be a detriment to your new church's outreach efforts. Don't sacrifice the eternal future of many for the present comfort of those already in the fold.

NEXT STEPS

APPLY TO YOUR SETTING

Examine your current church budget. Look at every line item and ask whether or not it helps the new church directly accomplish its mission and vision, as currently understood. Make adjustments as necessary.

Discover how much your new church currently spends on outreach and evangelism. Determine ways to increase the amount appropriated to this area of ministry.

Also find out how much the church is budgeting for missions involvement. Figure out ways to get more of your attendees participating in missions efforts locally and at a distance.

One more time, look at the current church budget and see how much of it is tied to "fixed" expenses (things that are committed long-term and don't allow for annual flexibility). Before you consider additional fixed expenses, determine how you will keep from compromising the evangelistic ministry of the church plant. Prepare accordingly.

Evaluate your calendar in the same above-mentioned ways, in order to make the most of the people and time resources at your discretion.

GOOD QUESTIONS TO ASK

1. How do our monies and activities align with our mission and vision as a new church? What changes are needed to produce better alignment and results?

2. What needs to be done—internally and externally—in order for us to keep the focus on outreach and evangelism?

3. What will it take to gain greater participation in the missions efforts of our church plant, both locally and abroad? Who will be permitted to participate?

4. Before we make the decision to add staff or secure a permanent facility, what "non-negotiables" do we need to determine for our budget and our calendar?

5. What would unbiased outsiders say we value most, if they were to analyze our new church solely on an evaluation of our budget and calendar?

6. Why do we do what we do?

DIGGING DEEPER

Agee, Bill. *Church Planting.* Canton, GA: Marvik Church Solutions, 2011.

Griffith, Jim and Easum, Bill. *Ten Most Common Mistakes Made by New Church Starts.* St. Louis, MO: Chalice Press, 2008.

Nebel, Tom and Rohrmayer, Gary. *Church Planting Landmines.* Carol Stream, IL: ChurchSmart Resources, 2005.

Schuller, Robert H. *Your Church Has a Fantastic Future!* Ventura, CA: Regal Books, 1986.

Stetzer, Ed. *Planting Missional Churches.* Nashville, TN: Broadman & Holman Publishers, 2006.

9

In the Community

It was a Saturday and Pastor Joe, along with a significant slice of his congregation, was out at the soccer fields in town. For two seasons each year, the children's league held multiple games here on the weekend. The league was always looking for volunteers to help. It's not hard to figure out why; the crowds were usually large, with so many families in the town involved.

The church family at Redemption Fellowship saw it as an invitation, a welcomed opportunity to serve others in the community by living the Gospel before "the eyes of their world," as one of them put it. They had been taught by Pastor Joe to look for ways to "take the Gospel out to the people where they are, rather than wait for them to come to us."

"We live in a world where, in most people's eyes, we must earn the right to be heard," he had said. "That goes for almost anything we say, but certainly, in regards to the Gospel. If it is as life-changing as we say, we have to show it to a world that desperately needs to see the difference Jesus makes. They think we're just peddling religion; they need to know that it's so much more—a life-giving relationship with the living God. For them to know —really know —this truth, most of them will have to see it evidenced in our lives."

From the beginning, the new church determined to be "visible" in the community. In one sense, it helped that they weren't able to depend upon their own building and signage to do that for them. Additionally, it seemed an advantage not to limit their visibility to one location in town. "We will have to make our own visibility by getting out among the people," Pastor Joe said. And get out among them they did!

The soccer games were just one place where Redemption Fellowship was helping out. Joe had gone to see the mayor and other key civic leaders not long after his arrival in town and had learned several ways the young church could be a blessing to the townspeople. The leadership of the new church had determined they would focus on only two specific things they could do in the beginning, but they would do them well.

"Our responsibility doesn't stop here," he said. "We must be intentional in the way we use our time. This starts with us all recognizing our responsibility to our families and then to our neighbors who live around us." Pastor Joe encouraged them to find ways to strengthen those relationships and to find generous and unselfish ways to serve these people whom God had placed so close in their daily lives.

"Cultivate opportunities with co-workers, too, and even acquaintances whom you encounter regularly: bank tellers, gas station attendants, checkout clerks at stores, etc." Becoming intentional in the use of time with others would make a difference for Christ later.

Pastor Joe practiced what he preached. He found ways to grow relationships with his neighbors, including Bill next door, who was an avid NASCAR fan like himself, and the Stevens couple across the street, who enjoyed experimenting with exotic food menus. He also took former classmate, Rick, to a ball game recently and began new relationships with Ken, a mechanic who worked on his cars over the past six months, and Dr. Hernandez, the new dentist he discovered when he moved back to town.

"After all," Pastor Joe reminded his congregation, "Jesus told us to 'GO and MAKE DISCIPLES,' that's our job; we'll leave it up to Him to encourage them to 'COME and SEE.'"

Epic Community Church in Aberdeen, Maryland, started in 2010, with a vision God placed in the heart of church planter Brian Watts, and his parent congregation, Oak Grove Baptist Church. Over the next year, Brian and the core group of leaders who would help him launch Epic Church took seriously this part of their calling: to get into the community and serve it. They looked for the perfect way to live out this calling and to demonstrate to the people of Aberdeen that their presence was to help people through the love and opportunity God had given them. As a result, before they even held their first worship service, the new church partnered with Habitat for Humanity in building a house for a needy family in the community. In fact, Epic went so far as to become the primary sponsor for the couple who would inhabit the new dwelling. They ministered to them, supported them and put love in action for their benefit. They wanted to show this family—and the community, at large—that their new church was present to make a difference, for Jesus' sake.

> It should be obvious, but it's apparently not. The church is supposed to get out of its "building" and into the community.

It should be obvious, but it's apparently not. The church is supposed to get out of its "building" and into the community. It is not meant to remain inside, keeping to itself; rather, it is to "go and make disciples," a never-ending, incarnational (literally meaning, "in the flesh") ministry among the people. This is the heart of the Great Commission, even as it was the essential characteristic of our Lord's ministry itself (John 1:14).

Church plants have a built-in advantage here; almost none of them have their own building in the early days of their ministry. In fact, a wide majority of them don't even have access to any facility "24/7" during their first year or two of existence. This evident "obstacle" may, in reality, be an advantage for their growth and expansion. Without an on-going place to call "home," the community itself becomes the place where the church "pitches its tent" during almost every hour of the week.

This has other advantages, too, both in motivating the attendees and in reaching those not yet reached. It creates a mindset that thinks beyond the "walls" of the church. It requires the new church to engage the community, not hide from it. And as we have already seen, it provides the rationale for a larger budget and calendar priority that extends beyond insiders who are a part of the new church already.

KNOW YOUR COMMUNITY

New churches have to connect two pieces of information in order for them to function effectively: they must know what makes the community "tick," and they must know why their new church exists. We have addressed the understanding of purpose and mission elsewhere in this book; here we will focus on the necessity of knowing your community.

The goal is to discover and assess the needs of one's community. Several key components usually assist church planters in determining these things. First, planters must become proficient in analyzing and deciphering demographic information and statistics about the community. They scour these reports, looking for keys to the community's viability, the changes happening, the strengths and potential needs within it. They explore the community, both to confirm through their senses the truths of what they've found, but also to uncover additional nuggets of value not usually evidenced in a statistical analysis. They will also study the rhythms and relationships of the community, observing the habits and patterns of behavior within it, as well as interviewing and dialoguing with the key leaders there (e.g., political leaders, business leaders, educational leaders and religious leaders, among others).

New churches will compile this information and compare it to their own understanding of the mission that has brought them into being. Where these two things—community need and church purpose—collide, there the new church will attempt to implement a strategy that makes a difference in the community.

Since the church is new to the community, it is not uncommon for the planter and other leaders to put the community under a microscope. They have little or no frame of reference with which to begin, so they make very few assumptions. They let their senses share with their heart and head what is missing or needed, so that the new church can focus its early energies on impacting the community at these points of leverage.

GO, NOT COME (ONLY) STRATEGY

There is an ongoing debate among church planters about whether the way to grow an effective church is through incarnational (the church goes to the people) ministry or through attractional (the people come to the church) ministry. Both sides have vocal and passionate advocates. In truth, a combination of both is likely true. However, my personal opinion is that a preponderance of the efforts should be found in the "going" part of ministry. We are long past the day (if it truly ever existed) when a church can simply "hang out its shingle," announce it is here and then expect people to show up on the weekend for worship. Rather, the community has often come to think of the church in terms like "irrelevant," "hypocritical," "judgmental," "fanatics," "self-absorbed," etc. Planters realize that to reclaim some of the lost reputation of the church, it needs to be the ones who go to those within the community and encounter them on "their home turf." It is presumptuous to assume otherwise.

> "Acts of kindness" keep Christ-followers "centered" on humility and service, key characteristics in Jesus' own ministry.

Planters, out of necessity, passion and logic, understand they must build an outreach strategy that goes where the people are and acts lovingly toward them in their most natural habitat. So, they plan activities at homes, in the neighborhoods, in the parks, at events or in other public spaces for all people in town. In addition, they will make themselves available for service to residents in a variety of different ways. All of this is an effort to intersect with people who live in the community and "show" them the love of Jesus.

Steve Sjogren has become synonymous with this kind of service activity. His passion for "acts of kindness" has produced a Pied Piper influence on most church planters today. Steve first shared about this "incarnational" ministry engagement with the community in Cincinnati, Ohio, where he joined God in planting the Cincinnati Vineyard Fellowship. He has continued it in the subsequent ministry efforts of his current church, which he also planted, in Tampa, Florida. Sjogren believes strongly in the "credibility factor" such ministry earns. But he also believes that "acts of kindness" keep Christ-followers "centered" on humility and service, key characteristics in Jesus' own ministry.[43]

SOCIAL GOSPEL?

Beyond Sjogren, other writers, including David Wheeler, have chosen to retitle these acts of kindness under the banner of "servant evangelism."[44] At times, it has drawn criticism as a simple rebranding of the old "social gospel." However, in a day when social justice issues are high priorities in the hearts and minds of most church planters, new church starters have a tendency to believe that Jesus and His teachings are holistic and should impact our behavior toward the entirety of the human experience, not simply a spiritual "conversion."

> Incarnational, servant evangelism is largely a seed-sowing ministry that is necessary before much of the harvest can be reaped.

Today, when the church is under suspicion in society by some for its sinful (embezzlement, sex scandals, etc.) behavior, such acts of service are more needed than ever. The North American Mission Board of the Southern Baptist Convention, for example, has kept its emphasis on Disaster Relief—currently the third largest relief aid agency in the United States—because it demonstrates additional life concerns, not solely for the souls of men, but for their comprehensive well-being, too. It is an expression of "a cup of cold water in Jesus' name," dressed in contemporary clothing. In fact, the North American Mission Board has gone so far as to name its servant evangelism initiative "Love Loud," out of the hope and dream the ministry will demonstrate Christ's call for His people to *"Love your neighbor as yourself"* (Matthew 22:39). This emphasis rings true with most church planters and is used effectively to penetrate their community and respond to its needs, as they can.

In this way, such incarnational efforts are framed not simply as "an end," the goal of the planter and his new church; rather, they serve as a "means," too, in that they are the groundwork for further opportunities to share the Gospel and "make disciples." As Ben Arment has noted, there are really only two seasons in the life of a new church: sowing seeds and bringing in the harvest.[45] Incarnational, servant evangelism is largely a seed-sowing ministry that is necessary before much of the harvest can be reaped.

EARNING CREDIBILITY

There are additional caveats that planters gain from taking the message of Christ to the streets and living it out before the eyes of their community. First, it legitimizes a new work in the community. Second, it builds significant relationships.

The efforts to help others in town, especially when community leaders have shared these needs or opportunities with the new church, are huge eye-openers to many residents. The perceptions that "the church is a critic of the community," "churches seek favorable treatment from city leaders" and "the church only cares for itself" are neutralized by such behavior. It lowers the defenses of skeptics and provides an "engraved invitation" to show the love of Christ in action to the rest of the community. It makes a marked impression on those who are served, and often on observers, as well. In this way, it legitimizes the presence—and message—of the new church in the community. It adds clout to its existence and makes others aware of its presence.

This can hardly be overestimated in importance. One of the largest barriers a new church must overcome is the fact that most people in the community are ignorant of its presence. Even those plants that use heavy marketing saturation techniques find a great percentage of the community residents have "filtered out" their efforts to be known. However, action offered to help those in need, or to improve and better the community in which both groups—residents and new church members—live, is noticed, appreciated and can often lead to something more.

These newfound, grateful residents are now often open to a relationship that begins to form around the common concerns and values of things that make the community special and unique to them. They have found allies who desire to make their "hometown" better. Public officials, civic leaders and other "gatekeepers" fall into this pattern, as well, for the effective planter and his new church will have discovered some of the ways they can help serve the community from these significant community people. Their efforts typically lead to opportunities for both parties to know each other better and to share life in a larger context. For the new church, it affords an opportunity to validate their care and concern for the people where God has planted them. They will have earned the credibility to minister among the people, because the community will see their love and sacrifice on the behalf of others.

SERVING AS WELL AS SHARING

This in no way dismisses the need for church plants or their leaders to share the Good News verbally. Rather, it endorses the need. And it will likely increase the opportunities, especially those that will take place in a natural, rather than artificial, contrived way.

There is a great scene illustrating this in the movie, *Back to the Future*. In the movie, Marty McFly has been transported back to 1955, the time when his parents first met. As he is discovering his new surroundings, he spots a Texaco "service station," or what we would call simply a gas station today. The movie illustrates the difference: while Marty is looking, a car drives up and FOUR attendants come out to help...one pumps the gas, one checks the oil, one cleans the windshield and one checks the tires. Marty is bewildered. I think it's because he's seeing exaggerated service in action, something entirely foreign to him at a "gas station" in his world.

New churches elicit the same reaction through incarnational ministry in their community. Incredulity gives ways to appreciation. Appreciation leads to potential relationship. Relationship leads to opportunity to share the Gospel. Sharing the Gospel finds receptive hearts because the hearer knows the sharer cares.

Genuine service is not manipulative; it is authentic love in action. Church planters who lead their church in such incarnational community efforts will make it a regular part of the lifestyle of their new church, not simply an event on the calendar. While collectively they will engage in community activity regularly, attendees and members are taught to practice it personally in their own neighborhoods, as well. Service starts at home.

> Genuine service is not manipulative; it is authentic love in action.

And when genuine service is seen in the name of Christ, it begs the question about motivation. Time after time, new church volunteers will be asked, "Why are you doing this?" And time and time again, they have the opportunity to share the love of Christ, both in a practical, relevant way through service and in a verbal, loving way through the sharing of the Good News of Jesus Christ and what He has done for each one of them.

NEXT STEPS

APPLY TO YOUR SETTING

Exegete your community. Study demographics and psychographics. Walk or drive slowly through it. Do the same with your new church congregation, studying the statistics and people involved. Examine where they overlap. Build ministry where they intersect.

Set up appointments to meet with key community leaders, including the mayor, councilpersons, police chief, fire chief and school superintendent. Learn from them the needs of the community as they understand them. Find ways your new church can help meet one or two of these needs.

Evaluate the servant evangelism strategy of your church plant. Note the initiatives used, the locations cultivated and the results seen. Don't leave the "same" location too soon; you're building relationships and familiarity. Conserve the results.

Train your people to serve, starting at home with their neighbors and co-workers. Have them equipped to share the Good News naturally, starting with their own story, when given the chance.

GOOD QUESTIONS TO ASK

1. How would we describe our community? What makes it unique? What are its needs?

2. Who do we need to meet to learn about the life and concerns of our city? What will we do with what we learn? What needs will we help meet?

3. What is our intentional corporate servant evangelism strategy? How will we evaluate its success?

4. What is our intentional personal servant evangelism strategy? How will we evaluate its success?

5. What adjustments in our calendar and budget may be necessary to make the most of these incarnational evangelism efforts?

DIGGING DEEPER

Arment, Ben. *Church in the Making.* Nashville, TN: Broadman & Holman Publishing, 2010.

Campolo, Tony and Aeschliman, Gordon. *101 Ways Your Church can Change the World.* Ventura, CA: Regal Books, 1993.

Earley, Dave and Wheeler, David. *Evangelism Is...* Nashville, TN: Broadman & Holman Publishing, 2010.

Rusaw, Rick and Swanson, Eric. *The Externally-Focused Church.* Loveland, CO: Group Publishing, 2004.

Sjogren, Steve. *101 Ways to Reach Your Community.* Colorado Springs, CO: NavPress, 2001.

10

Limited Structure

"The structure of a church should be similar to the skeleton that gives structure to your body," Pastor Joe shared with his leadership team. "It should be functional, but not draw attention to itself. Too much structure and it becomes the focus of attention; too little structure and the body can't accomplish what it is intended to do."

"That sounds great, Pastor," chimed in one of the leaders, "but how do we develop a structure that does that for this new church?"

"Great question," Joe replied. "It's certainly more difficult than it sounds. It starts with a few assumptions. For one thing, form ought to follow function, wouldn't you agree? In other words, we don't just have something in our structure because other churches have it; rather, we have it because it helps us in what we are on mission here to do.

"Second, less is typically more. What I mean by this is that we humans have a tendency to keep on adding to what we have in place, and rarely ever subtract things that are no longer needed. Ministries are always growing, policies are inevitably expanding and administration is often enlarged. The result is more complexity, which can lead to stagnation. On the other hand, a nimble, dynamic structure allows us to respond quickly to the new opportunities God may send our way."

"That makes sense, at least in theory," another of the members said. "But how do we make that reality?"

"Well, that leads me to a final assumption," Pastor Joe replied. "Redemption Fellowship will function best when we live like a family, rather than a business. Families emphasize each person's passions, strengths and maturity. Churches ought to enable *members to serve out of these areas, as well. In fact, I hope it will be said of Redemption Fellowship someday that we are a permission-giving family, not a boundary-restricting business. Let's structure the new church, so that people don't have to worry about running into 'tripwires.' Let's find ways to bless them and the desire God has ignited in their hearts for ministry."*

Too much structure has the ability to stifle potential growth and development for any church, especially in the early days of its existence.

There, I said it. My bias is showing. Perhaps no other issue can cause more damage to a new church than an over-abundance of structure.

What do I mean by structure? Typically, it is evident in the organization of church life. This is seen in titles and roles. It is seen in policies and procedures. It is manifest in flow charts and organizational charts, business meetings and manuals instructing the church on how to live out its existence.

To be sure, all elements of structure are not bad. All groups need structure to move from chaos to community, from disarray to design. When functional, organization is a wonderful thing. It enables focus on mission, forward movement collectively and effective, decisive action. The problem is that in most churches structure and organization are dysfunctional, or they have become dysfunctional. Most churches don't even know why they do what they do; sadly, they just do it.

> Most churches don't even know why they do what they do; sadly, they just do it.

Form must follow function.

Structure cannot, and should not, exist for the sake of structure. It must have a "why" for its existence; it must support the mission of the church.

New churches get this, most often intuitively at first. With little or no "formal" organization or structure at the beginning, they flourish in a sea of chaos. Over the early months, they recognize the inherent need for some organization to take place, and as a result, add elements that are needed.

But what elements should be added, and when, becomes the difficult questions with which they grapple in the first couple of years. Bob Dale, in his book *To Dream Again*, acknowledges that the growth curve of a church begins to level out after an emphasis on organization and structure is added to church life.[46] The potential problem it presents is this: once organization and structure are added, management of the same organization takes precedence for many church leaders over outreach. Maintenance becomes operative, instead of innovation. And maintenance is the "kiss of death" in terms of growth.

Adding structure to the new church is more an art than a science.

There's no one right way to do it; however, wrong ways will quickly kill whatever momentum a new church may have. Why? It is because too much structure—or the wrong structure—controls the momentum, rather than conducts it. The difference can be fatal.

K.I.S.S. (aka, Less is More)

Church plants are born out of chaos. They thrive in this same chaos. They grow dramatically during these early days. For this to happen, church leaders have to be comfortable with such chaos. It requires ambiguity.

Unfortunately, most churches—and the pastors they select—are not comfortable with ambiguity, and they certainly don't like chaos. They want to have all the answers, even to anticipate all the questions they might address. To put it another way, they want to fill in the gaps in their understanding, so they won't be anxious regarding the unknown. This is the nature of security, a value most human beings embrace with passion. Rules and regulations provide such security; they give boundaries. Policies and procedures enable the gaps to be completed and the answers understood. They provide a safe, standard way to guide the entire process and the decisions it will produce.

This is not bad, in and of itself. In fact, boundaries are good and even necessary. However, the corollary "more boundaries (i.e., rules, procedures, etc.) lead to more security" is not helpful or needful in a new church's life. It prematurely truncates the growth cycle of the church plant and "ages" the church too quickly. In essence, the new church doesn't "act its age;" it attempts to act older.

This is a problem evidenced in many, if not most, church plants: they have a desire to "grow up" too quickly. They fantasize about being a "full service" church from early days in the life of their plant. They believe that when they organize the structure of church life ("what we will do") along with the means to handle it ("how we will do it"), then they'll be on their way toward long-term success.

They sacrifice ambiguity for security.

Unfortunately, those who do, find the security to be fleeting and often, nothing more than a mirage. The best church planters embrace the ambiguity of the time and revel in it. They keep the new church focused on the "why" of their existence before they concern themselves with the "what" or the "how." They act their age.

> The best church planters embrace the ambiguity of the time and revel in it.

I encountered a church plant during my second year in Maryland that didn't seem to grasp this. They were anxious to get "all their ducks in a row." They had just started public worship and three months later were ready to name officers (elders and deacons) and adopt a 26-page Constitution and Bylaws (that's right, 26 pages!!!). The Bylaws detailed what the church would do (programs and events) and how they would see ministry done (twenty-plus committees were named and described in the document). When asked how many people they currently had, the church planter indicated there were about thirty-five, and that included children. I challenged him on the need for such "organization" at this stage of his new church's development, but his response to me was, "We want to be ready for what's to come." Unfortunately, his plant stalled soon after, and while it lasted about five years, it never regained a growth momentum that made such structure necessary.

The key to organization in effective new churches is limited structure: not too much and not too little. Effective church planters desire—and the need of the church is—to keep it simple (K.I.S.S., i.e., "keep it simple, stupid"), especially in the earliest years. Add what is needed only when it is needed and when it easily supports the "why" of the new church. And don't ever add to the structure before your people within the church see the need for it! Most church members are wired for security; they want structure to help them feel protected and safe. So, if they're not asking for more structure, leaders ought to wait longer. They will ask soon enough.

FAMILY OR BUSINESS?

As an entity, churches tend to function more like a family or a business. The larger the church, the more likely it is to function like a business. The overwhelming number of people make it hard to accomplish anything "decently and in order" without structured processes. This makes sense. The need for order and structure tend to promote a business approach to the way the Western world conceptualizes the church experience.

The problem is "business" is never an analogy used for the church in the Scripture. "Family," "body," "flock," "building," "field:" these all are used. With the exception of "building," used once in 1 Corinthians 3:9, all of them are organic, living entities. One of these analogies involves a recognized group of people in relationship with each other: that is, the family. Perhaps this is our biggest clue to how a church can best be structured.

Within a family, all members have a role and responsibilities. These roles are both inherent (based on who we are: father, mother, child) and assigned (based on what we do: earn a paycheck, raise children, do chores, etc.). Some things are naturally obvious in such an entity: leadership in the family falls to the parents, not the children. Older ones, those with experience, have a responsibility to help the younger ones. All have something to do—certain responsibilities—but these are not the same. They are defined by the needs of the family and the abilities (or gifting) of the family member.

In family life, there is no need for manuals, committees or formal procedures to get most things done. Families function on the basis of roles and relationships. Some structure is needed, but it is limited. For churches, what is most needed is spelled out in Acts and in the Epistles, especially Paul's Pastoral Epistles to Timothy and Titus. Beyond that, structure has the potential to limit growth of the Body more than enhance it.

> What do these things have in common—committees, *Robert's Rules of Order*, policy and procedures manuals, organizational charts, constitution and bylaws, and even voting? The answer: none of them is mentioned in the Bible.

Here is a question for you: what do these things have in common—committees, *Robert's Rules of Order*, policy and procedures manuals, organizational charts, constitution and bylaws, and even voting? The answer: none of them is mentioned in the Bible. Yet, they are very common experiences in most American churches. Perhaps not so surprisingly, the younger the church is, the less likely they will have any of these things. And the younger the church, the greater likelihood it is growing. Coincidence? I think not.

Now, it may sound like I'm suggesting a new church not have any "business-like" characteristics. Nothing could be further from the truth. There must be boundaries and processes; these need to be known by all participants. Order is necessary for efficiency. I am simply advocating for a simpler, more dynamic and adaptable structure, that values relationships more than the process, allows for quick response to ministry opportunities and edifies the Body in a non-divisive way.

TO BLESS OR TO CURSE?

Limited structure means accentuating the opportunities to give permission to members of the church family, rather than restrict them from taking initiative. This is huge. Setting boundaries for what can and can't be done is good, if safety and security are needed. However, if you want disciples and members to be creative, active and engaged, encourage them to think outside the box. (That means you can't give them "a box" to examine in the first place!) Give them freedom to roam in their imagination, to allow the Spirit to lead them down new paths and to discover unexamined opportunities.

It means finding a way to say "yes" whenever possible.

The ones in your church who won't like this are often the leaders. The "bean counters" don't like this; they want everything tied up neatly, with a nice bow on top. The "controllers" don't like it either; it threatens them and their leadership by allowing members the freedom to do beyond

> Rules breed conformity; conformity breeds complacency.

what these leaders desire. These are the "task-driven" people in your church. They are the "doers." They want structure; they feel like everybody needs an abundance of structure, which often translates into rules and regulations. They are often your volunteers (because they're "doers!"). They are eager to help...on their own terms. They want to get rid of ambiguity. They want to move the process along. So they create systems, policies and procedures. (In their mind, these equal "rules" most of the time.)

Rules breed conformity; conformity breeds complacency.

The negative nature of such regulations will snuff the life right out of the relational dimension so vital to an early church's life and so significant to its attendees. Relationships are the primary advantage every new church has over any established church; why would one be so eager to give that up?

Enable people to dream, to discover, to explore. This happens in churches that seek to bless, not to curse. They find ways to say "yes" to their people, and essentially, to the Spirit of God as He moves on their hearts. The alternative is to bog members down in procedures that must be followed or permissions that must be given. While this perhaps may follow the "letter of the law," such an attitude kills the spirit of those most excited and passionate about what God is doing in their midst, and in their own individual lives.

Complexity—more rules—results in two things: bureaucracy and less freedom. Bureaucracy leads to inaction; it paralyzes activity. It stalls forward motion and keeps individuals from the possibility of joining God in an opportune moment. In such a system, decision-making processes require too many permissions, too long of a time, and too often lead to no decision at all. In addition, more complexity restricts the freedom the individual or group has. It encroaches on one's own ability to *"follow the Spirit"* (Galatians 5:25). The results are often confusion, frustration and eventually, apathy.

New, young churches are always on the lookout for new servants. As a result, they are eager to find ways to encourage individual participation and service soon after arrival. Sure, there are necessary precautions and concerns that must be addressed; due diligence is always required. But church plants look for ways to say "yes" whenever they can, just like a parent affirming and encouraging a child to grow into the calling God has for him or her.

PLACEMENT, NOT NOMINATION OR ELECTION

One way this is happening in new churches is through a reversal of the volunteer leader process. In many established churches, over the previous decades leaders have been nominated and elected to positions and committees in church business meetings. This process apparently follows a procedure set forth in *Robert's Rules of Order*, the consensus "book of order" on how churches are to conduct their corporate business together.[47]

In some churches, this no doubt works effectively; in others I've observed, however, it leaves gaps in leadership that the congregation and its leaders feel obligated to "fill." (Most don't even ask the "why" question regarding the position; they're simply worried about the "whom!") Leaders responsible for this assignment start with the best potential worker in their estimation. However, if that person says "no," they will move on and on until they find someone who is simply willing to accept the responsibility. They rarely—if ever—ask about the skills or gifting necessary for someone willing to assume the position in question.

This can lead to some very unfortunate and misguided behavior. Church members are "guilted" or "shamed" into taking a position they are not shaped to fill. They may be cajoled, manipulated or embarrassed in the process. And for the member willing to accept the responsibility, he or she may feel frustrated and unfulfilled. This can lead to quick burnout and the unwillingness to accept another responsibility later in life, which obviously has consequences for one's own discipleship.

New churches, on the contrary, are more and more reversing this process. They are starting with the belief that God is sending specific people to the church for His reason, and it is the new church's job to help everyone involved determine what that reason may be. It means learning how God has shaped these persons for service: what are their gifts and temperament, their skills and experience? It also means knowing what is needed (gifts, temperament, etc.) in each ministry opportunity the church currently offers. Furthermore, it means a willingness to "suspend" or "close" a ministry opportunity when there is no appropriate leader or the willingness to "open" new ministries that fit the gifting of a person God has brought to serve in the new church.

When this happens, new churches place these individuals in ministry settings that fit the way God has made them. This results in workers who are fulfilled and joyful in their work. It motivates other potential workers to commit as willing volunteers, knowing the new church is going to take seriously who they are and their needs on the path to maturity. It leads to less frustration and burnout from workers.

But it's not easy. It requires new churches to have a flexible and fluid organization. It has to be adaptable and dynamic in how it is structured to do ministry over time, based on whom God is leading to be a part of the congregation (and whom He may be moving away via job transfers, death, etc.). Yet, part of the effectiveness of new churches happens because the leadership involved is willing to do the hard work of shaping the church the way they perceive God is leading them. They seek to impact their world most effectively, not simply the way they personally prefer or the way it was done in previous years. They know that limited structure leaves the least encumbrance and hassle. It enables them to adjust the Body of Christ, so that it is moving where the Head, Jesus Himself, is leading them to go.

They never forget the "why" in what they do.

NEXT STEPS

APPLY TO YOUR SETTING

Examine the structure, policies and procedures already at work within your new church. Ask why you have these things in place and what purpose they accomplish. Make sure that form follows function.

Determine whether you use a familial, business or some other framework for how your church functions together. Examine it in line with biblical teachings. A good rule of thumb is always: follow the teaching of God's Word when commands are explicit; use discretion where only opinions or stories are offered.

Analyze the people of your church to learn their gifting, passions and "shape" for ministry. In light of your new church's mission and vision, adjust your ministry efforts accordingly.

Decide how to keep your structure as dynamic, simple, flexible, fluid and adaptable as possible.

GOOD QUESTIONS TO ASK

1. What processes, policies and procedures are necessary and what are simply desirable? What makes the difference?

2. How are decisions made in our church? What role do members play in the process?

3. How does our organizational framework conform to the teachings of the Word of God? What other influences are causing us to "do what we do?"

4. How are we discovering what God is sending our way in the form of new attendees and members? What implications for ministry does this present us as a church?

5. *How can we better structure ourselves as the Body of Christ, so that we "follow the Spirit," not getting ahead of Him or lagging behind?*

DIGGING DEEPER

Allen, Roland. *Missionary Methods: St. Paul's or Ours?* Grand Rapids, MI: Eerdmans, 1962.

Dale, Tony & Felicity and Barna, George. *The Rabbit and the Elephant.* Brentwood, TN: BarnaBooks, 2009.

Moore, Ralph. *Starting a New Church.* Ventura, CA: Regal Books, 2002.

Murray, Stuart. *Church Planting.* Carlisle, Cumbria, UK: Paternoster Press, 1998.

Rainey, Joel. *Planting Churches in the Real World.* 2nd edition. Smyrna, DE: Missional Press, 2012.

PLANTED
Starting Well, Growing Strong

Epilogue

"God has been good to us," Pastor Joe declared to the Redemption Fellowship congregation as he started his sermon at the fifth anniversary celebration of the church. "Who would have imagined we would have experienced God's blessing and abundance like we have over these past five years? God has moved in our midst and the congregation is growing by leaps and bounds. No doubt, much of this can be credited to the fact we have stayed close to God and His mission for us. We have remained focused on the harvest field. As a result, we continue to move boldly into God's future for us. What could be better or more satisfying than that?

"We started this church with an evangelistic desire to impact the dear people of our town for our Lord Jesus. Many of you are here today because God used us to do just that. And now, additionally through the churches we have planted—Mercy House and GracePoint—we are seeing the influence of our lives multiplied exponentially throughout the region. Hundreds of people are in the Kingdom today because Redemption Fellowship exists to make disciples and in turn, to send them out. I, for one, can't wait to see what God has in store for us in the days and years to come!

"Now take your Bibles and turn with me to our text for this morning's message as we celebrate God's goodness to us, His people..."

Pastor Joe and Redemption Fellowship have illustrated for us the evangelistic reasons why new churches grow so dramatically during the early years of their existence. Though they had the obstacles of every new "start up" (lack of personnel, funding, awareness, etc.), they also experienced the dynamics of spiritual warfare and the sins of the soul that challenged them. Only through the power of the Holy Spirit were they able to plant a church at all; He has always been the only One who can bring "the church" to life!

Why God chooses to involve us in His story of redemption is beyond comprehension. Perhaps it is because we are the best example, the authentic representation, of His redemptive grace at work. His life in and through us—if we exhibit that life as we should—draws others to Him.

New churches turn their obstacles into opportunities. It forces them into the community, to budget more for outreach and discipleship, to invest in relationships, to stay focused on the mission God has given them. These things, which we have elaborated here, in turn sharpen the work they seek to do and if done well, produce highly evangelistic new churches.

> These advantages are in essence "time stamped," meaning the early years of a church plant's ministry afford the greatest opportunity for these principles to be put in play.

NEXT STEPS FOR CHURCH PLANTS

Any new church can capitalize on these opportunities, if they attempt to do so. The key is an unwavering commitment to evangelism and discipleship throughout the process. From the planter who leads the new effort to the structure itself that sustains the work, the intention must be to reach the lost effectively with the Good News of Jesus Christ. Leaders need to pursue this focused commitment in an unrelenting fashion. The longer these elements serve as motivations for the new church's purpose, the more effective it will be. Other motivations in church planting will reveal themselves over time for what they truly are.

As noted above, these advantages are in essence "time stamped," meaning the early years of a church plant's ministry afford the greatest opportunity for these principles to be put in play. If implemented effectively, they cascade as momentum is built. Moreover, they imprint the new church with values and habits that can extend its growth-bearing years further into the future than those without such DNA. They enable the church to have far-reaching, multiplying Kingdom impact.

The greatest advantage new churches have over established ones is found in the power of relationships. Established churches can offer facilities and programs, often with bigger budgets and staffs to support them. New churches rarely find themselves with any of these things to offer unreached people. Rather, they offer the personal and authentic power of relationships—love, care, attention and acceptance—and a desire for the new church to experience the strength of genuine, biblical community, where interdependence, sacrifice and servanthood are the order of the day. New churches that maximize the relational quotient will keep their momentum moving forward into the future.

A word of caution is in order, too: resist the desire to be a "full service" church as long as you can. What do I mean by this? Don't give in to the urge to provide all the programs, events and activities other more established churches provide. Put off the purchase of a permanent facility as long as you are able. Limit the addition of other full-time staffers until absolutely necessary. And don't do any of these things until after your new church has begun reproducing other churches first. Otherwise, the Kingdom-dream of multiplying churches from your own church—the most effective evangelistic methodology under heaven—may never become a reality, at all.

NEXT STEPS FOR ESTABLISHED CHURCHES

Can established churches learn from these principles? Undoubtedly, they can. However, the journey is more precipitous, due to other circumstances that impact their existence. Navigation of these obstacles is dangerous and nerve-racking.

Many a good man has lost his footing on the jagged cliffs of possibility, because he has neglected to recognize the ground giving way beneath him! Such efforts must be bathed in prayer, supported by key leaders already within the church and finessed with biblical authority and counsel each step of the way. For established churches willing to make the journey, the adventure will be rich indeed.

If successful in implementing these changes, any established church has the potential to move forward in growth again, or at a higher level than previously experienced. But in reality, the component that will determine whether a church attempts such efforts will depend not upon the knowledge they glean or possess; rather, it will depend upon their heart and volition, married to a risk-taking faith in Almighty God, *"who is able to do above and beyond all that we ask or think according to the power that works in us—to Him be glory in the church and in Christ Jesus to all generations, forever and ever. Amen"* (Ephesians 3:20-21).

NOTES

Introduction

[1] Rick Warren, *The Purpose-Driven Life*, Grand Rapids, MI: Zondervan, pp. 235, 246.

[2] C. Peter Wagner, *Church Planting for a Greater Harvest: A Comprehensive Guide*, Ventura, CA: Regal Books, 1990, p. 7f., 11, 16, 22, 24.

[3] Bruce McNichol, "Churches Die with Dignity," *Christianity Today*, Volume 36, January 14, 1991, p. 69.

[4] Larry Kreider, *House Church Networks: A Church for a New Generation*, Ephrata, PA: House to House Publications, 2001, p. 73, cites this from a report by the American Society for Church Growth, "Enlarging Our Borders," presented to the Executive Presbytery in January, 1999.

[5] Gerald Colbert, Joe Hernandez, Van Kicklighter and Steve Reid, *New Churches Needed: Our Church Can Help*, Alpharetta, GA: North American Mission Board of the Southern Baptist Convention, 2001, p. v in the Introduction material cite the Annual Church Profile of the churches within the Southern Baptist Convention in 1999 for this information.

[6] Christian A. Schwarz, *Natural Church Development: A Guide to Eight Essential Qualities of Healthy Churches*, St. Charles, IL: ChurchSmart Resources, 1996, p. 124f. cites this; his revised edition in 2006 shares along the same lines, pp. 72f., 48-50; Aubrey Malphurs, *Planting Growing Churches for the 21st Century*, Second Edition, Grand Rapids, MI: Baker Books, 1998, p. 44; Ed Stetzer, *Planting Missional Churches*, Nashville, TN: Broadman & Holman Publishers, 2006, p. 6, 33; http://www.namb.net/overview-why-send/, on the website of the North American Mission Board, Southern Baptist Convention, lists information on evangelistic effectiveness.

[7] NAMB's website, mentioned above, finds this information in the book by Ed Stetzer and Warren Bird, *Viral Churches*, San Francisco, CA: Jossey-Bass, 2010, p. 25.

[8] Tim Keller, *"Why Plant Churches?"* is a paper presented at Redeemer Presbyterian Church, 2003, p. 1. The occasion and audience of this paper are unknown to the author, but I am in possession of the document.

Chapter One – An Inspiring Leader

[9] John Maxwell, *The 21 Irrefutable Laws of Leadership*, Nashville, TN: Thomas Nelson, Inc., 1998, p. 11, cites this as the 2nd law of leadership, "the law of influence."

[10] Leon Morris, *The Gospel According to John*, The New International Commentary on the New Testament series, Grand Rapids, MI: William B. Eerdmans Publishing Company, 1971, p. 256, among others, cites this "necessity."

[11] According to the website http://spaceflight.nasa.gov/shuttle/reference/basics/ascent.html, "The shuttle consumed more than 1.59 million kilograms (3.5 million pounds) of fuel during its first 8 ½ minutes of flight." The site also states at http://spaceflight.nasa.gov/shuttle/reference/basics/launch.html, "The journey starts relatively slowly: at liftoff, the shuttle weighs more than 2.04 million kilograms (4.5 million pounds) and it takes eight seconds for the engines and boosters to accelerate the ship to 161 kilometers per hour (100 mph.) But by the time the first minute has passed, the shuttle is traveling more than 1,609 kilometers per hour (1,000 mph) and it has already consumed more than one and a half million pounds of fuel." These facts were posted on the NASA website as of March, 2013. If I am reading these facts correctly, then 3.5 million pounds of fuel in a 4.5 million pound shuttle is expended in the first 8 ½ minutes of flight, a total of 78% of its total weight.

[12] Carey first spoke these words in his sermon to the Baptist Association meeting in Northampton, England, on May 30, 1792, according to the website http://www.wmcarey.edu/carey/expect/.

[13] John Maxwell, *Leadership Promises for Every Day: A Daily Devotional*, Nashville, TN: J. Countryman, 2003, p. 245, the devotional thought for August 10.

[14] John Maxwell, *Developing the Leader Within You*, Nashville: Thomas Nelson, 1993, p. 21f.

Chapter Two - Calling and Motivation

[15] Roland H. Bainton, *Here I Stand: A Life of Martin Luther*, Nashville, TN: Pierce and Smith, 1950, p. 144.

[16] Mark Batterson, *In a Pit with a Lion on a Snowy Day: How to Survive and Thrive When Opportunity Roars*, Colorado Springs, CO: Multnomah Books, Chapter 1 "Locking Eyes with Your Lion," pp.9-19.

[17] Leland Ryken, *Worldly Saints: The Puritans as They Really Were* (Grand Rapids: Academie Books, 1986), 24f., 28, 229, cites Hugh Latimer and John Cotton on this, among others; in addition, Garth M. Rosell, Professor of Church History at Gordon-Conwell Theological Seminary, South Hamilton, Massachusetts, in "Call to Ministry: Some Historical Reflections," (Unpublished article, 2002), 8, mentions John Cotton too, but also includes Cotton Mather's comments on this.

[18] Gordon MacDonald, *Ordering Your Private World*, Nashville, TN: Thomas Nelson, Inc., 1985, chapter 3, "Caught in a Golden Cage," pp. 28-41.

[19] John Worcester, *Purpose-Driven Church Planting* materials at Southern Baptist Theological Seminary, 1999, shares about a Christian Church/Churches of Christ study of 66 church plants over a six-year period with the following results; the numbers are the attendance at that time mark when the planter exhibited the indicated characteristic:

High D:	72 (1 year)	181 (5.2 years)
High I:	98_(1 year)	174 (3.6 years)
High S:	38 (1 year)	_77 (6.3 years)
High C:	39 (1 year)	_71 (4.3 years)

[20] Larry E. McCrary, compiled the unpublished teaching manual to supplement the written self-discovery workbook entitled *Discovery Tools: Does God Want Me to be Involved in Church Planting?*, Alpharetta, GA: North American Mission Board of the Southern Baptist Convention, 2003. The cited reference in the teaching manual is on page 13.

Chapter Three – Vision and Focus

[21] Thomas Rainer and Eric Geiger, *Simple Church*, Nashville: Broadman and Holman Publishing, 2006, pp. 58-62, 109-134, 135, 197-226, say that four characteristics are necessary for churches to make progress toward the objective of spiritual growth (disciple-making): clarity, movement, alignment and focus.

[22] Rick Warren, *The Purpose Driven Church*, Grand Rapids: Zondervan, 1995, p. 111f., 392.

Chapter Four – Passion for Those without Jesus

[23] Pastor Joe's "dream" is inspired and adapted from the real "Seashore" dream/vision that Robert E. (Bob) Logan, co-author of *The Church Planter's Toolkit*, shares in *Beyond Church Growth* (Grand Rapids, MI: Fleming H. Revel, 1989), p. 9f.

[24] This quotation is attributed to William Temple, Archbishop of Canterbury, 1942-1944. The actual quote is this: *"The Church is the only society on earth that exists for the benefit of non-members."*

[25] Thom Rainer reported on this orally to the State Directors of Missions Fellowship at the LifeWay Summit in Nashville, Tennessee, December, 2007. In a subsequent email he stated that his report was based on research from a North American Mission Board study dating back to 2000 or 2001 on baptism or "re-baptisms." Richie Stanley at NAMB confirmed on the phone in March 2013 that there has not been an updated study by NAMB on this. However, he stated that the current 2011 ratio on new believer to church members in the SBC is 1:48.

[26] Lynne & Bill Hybels, *Rediscovering Church*, Grand Rapids, MI: Zondervan Publishing House, 1995, p. 186.

[27] Penn Gillette, YouTube video, http://www.youtube.com/watch?v=fa9JE_ZVL88, *"The Gift of a Bible"* posted by Nate Callaway on February 28, 2009.

[28] Lynn & Bill Hybels, *Rediscovering Church*, Grand Rapids, MI: Zondervan Publishing House, 1995, p. 172.

[29] Rick Warren, *The Purpose Driven Church*, Grand Rapids, MI: Zondervan, 1995, pp. 190-194.

[30] The Alpha program and its attendant supporting material, at least in its USA form, are found online at http://alphausa.org. An excellent overview of its strategy and impact can be found at http://www.religion-online.org/showarticle.asp?title=2965, posted as of March, 2013, "The ABC's of Faith," written by Debra Bendis and previously appearing in *The Christian Century*, March 9, 2004, pp. 22-27.

[31] Travis Snode cites Pastor Martin Wickens of the Baptists Committed to World Evangelism website, http://bcwe.org/2012/08/16/statistics-about-church-attendance-in-the-uk/, dated August 16, 2012 and still posted as of March, 2013, in which he notes that overall attendance is down by 18% and church membership by 6%. Bendis in the article cited directly above, dated 2004, suggests that Church Research finds that British churches using Alpha are gaining members at an average growth rate of 15 percent. However, at an Alpha training conference, leaders caution that this happens gradually, and only with [church] commitment to the program.

Chapter Five - Creativity and Innovation

[32] Kevin Trampe, *"Left or Right Brain?,"* http://www.angelfire.com/wi/2brains/, lists over 30 characteristics typical of predominately right-brained people, last updated January 14, 2010, and still posted as of March, 2013.

[33] Lynn & Bill Hybels, *Rediscovering Church*, Grand Rapids, MI: Zondervan Publishing House, 1995, pp. 36, 52, say about 250 kids formed the nucleus of the new church.

[34] George G. Hunter III, *How to Reach Secular People*, Nashville, TN: Abingdon Press, 1992, pp. 85-87, mentions these three barriers and adds a fourth for those already "in" the church: total commitment.

Chapter Six - The Power of Relationships

[35] Point of Grace, *The Whole Truth* CD, Nashville, TN: Word Records, 1995, track 11.

36 Nelson Searcy, *Fusion*, Ventura, CA: Regal, 2007, pp. 67, 119f.

37 Gary L. McIntosh, *Beyond the First Visit*, Grand Rapids, MI: Baker Books, 2006, p. 25, cites this from the work of Flavil R. Yeakley, Jr., *Why Churches Grow*, Nashville, TN: Christian Communications, 3rd edition, 1986, but no page number is given.

38 Elmer Towns, *FRIEND DAY Resource Packet with CDs*, Elkton, MD: Ephesians 4 Ministries/Church Growth Institute, 2011a. In this author's opinion, this is still one of the best and simplest strategies around, especially for church planters to use.

Chapter Seven – Kingdom Citizens

39 The Cooperative Program of the Southern Baptist Convention is detailed, including its history, how it works and its potential at http://www.cpmissions.net/2003/what%20is%20cp.asp, as of March 2013.

40 Henry T. Blackaby and Claude V. King, *Experiencing God*, Nashville, TN: Broadman & Holman Publishers, 1994, pp. 73-82.

Chapter Eight – Budget and Time Priorities

41 Steve Sjogren, *Conspiracy of Kindness*, Ann Arbor, MI: Vine Books, 1993, p. 21.

42 Rick Warren, *The Purpose-Driven Church*, Grand Rapids, MI: Zondervan, 1995, p. 46.

Chapter Nine - In the Community

43 Steve Sjogren, *Conspiracy of Kindness*, Ann Arbor, MI: Vine Books, 1993, p. 19. See also his section on "Personal Growth," in the book *Community of Kindness*, Ventura, CA: Regal, 2003, pp. 98-119.

44 Dave Early and David Wheeler, *Evangelism Is...: How to Share Jesus with Passion and Confidence*, Nashville, TN: B & H Academic Publishing Group, 2010, p. 300, where Wheeler writes a chapter on "Creating Opportunities for Gospel Conversations," discussing ministry evangelism and servant evangelism in a variety of forms.

45 Ben Arment, *Church in the Making: What Makes or Breaks a New Church before It Starts*, Nashville, TN: B & H Publishing Group, 2010,

p. 35, where the author suggests "cultivating and planting" as the two seasons in each church planting venture.

Chapter Ten - Limited Structure

[46] Robert Dale, *To Dream Again*, Nashville, TN: Broadman Press, 1981, is classic literature on this topic. Chapter 7, pp. 88-102, on "The Promise and Threat of Ministry" for the church at the summit of the Growth cycle is a must read. Note the top of page 96, especially.

[47] *Robert's Rules of Order*, New York, NY: Bantam Books, 1986. Note especially the sections dealing with committees and the selection of officers, pp. 80-93, 165-182.

ABOUT THE AUTHOR

James David Jackson (he prefers "David") has been in ministry since 1977, when he served as a student missionary to New Hampshire while in college. He has served God in the local church as a children's minister, youth minister, associate pastor, interim pastor, senior pastor and a church planter over the years. He has taught at both the university and the seminary levels. In addition, he has worked in collegiate student ministry and in denominational service at both the associational (district) level in Boston, Massachusetts, and at the state convention (regional) level in Maryland/Delaware, since 1998.

He is a Doctor of Ministry graduate of Gordon-Conwell Theological Seminary. His degree in Christian Leadership focused on "examining the call of church planters." He also has earned three additional degrees over the years.

In 1983 while still a seminary student and single, he served in Exeter, New Hampshire and worked with his mentor, Bob Brindle, to start Fellowship Baptist Church. Eight years later, he served as church planter when Christ Community Chapel came into being in Quincy, Massachusetts. In 1992, he went on to plant Community Baptist Church in Weymouth, Massachusetts, as well. Community then parented five other church plants over the next six years, all in the metropolitan Boston area, while he was there.

He was the primary author and editor of *PlantLIFE: Principles and Practices in Church Planting* in 2008. *PLANTED: Starting Well, Growing Strong* is his first solo writing effort.

David has been married to his gorgeous wife, Joyce, for the past twenty-seven years. They have three wonderful children: Sarah, Jonathan and Rebekah. They also have a West Highland Terrier named Ripken.

www.ingramcontent.com/pod-product-compliance
Lightning Source LLC
LaVergne TN
LVHW051835080426
835512LV00018B/2898